Table of Contents

Glimpsing *Titanic*

The time was shortly after midnight on September 1, 1985. Crew members aboard *Knorr* kept a close eye on video screens in the ship's control center. Murky images of the muddy ocean bottom glowed on every monitor. Everyone eagerly waited for a sign they were near *Titanic*.

For days Robert Ballard, the expedition's head scientist, and the crew had been watching for any hint they were close to the great ship. They were starting to lose hope. Would they ever find Titanic?

Then at 12:48 a.m., a metal object came into view. Could it have fallen from the huge ship as it sank? Hopes rose as more objects streamed past on the monitors. A few minutes after 1:00 a.m., a clear image of a boiler appeared. The crew jumped and cheered. Seventy-three years after Titanic sank to the bottom of the Atlantic Ocean, Ballard and his crew had discovered its final resting place.

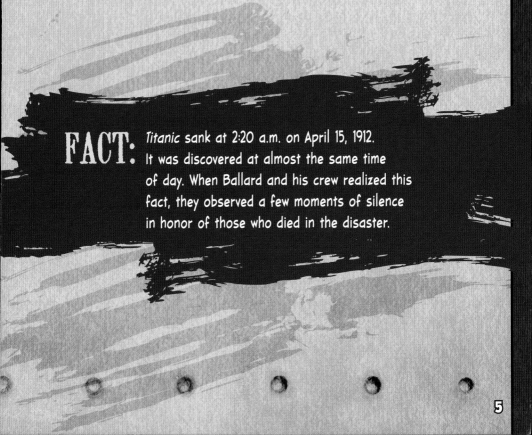

FACT: Titanic sank at 2:20 a.m. on April 15, 1912. It was discovered at almost the same time of day. When Ballard and his crew realized this fact, they observed a few moments of silence in honor of those who died in the disaster.

CHAPTER 1

Building *Titanic*

The Launch of 401

In the shipyard, workers often referred to the ship by its build number: 401. But everyone knew its name: *Titanic*. The name fit. It was the largest ocean liner of its time.

For two years 401 grew in size. Day by day, piece by piece, workers added more and more parts to the ship.

On May 31, 1911, bands played as thousands of people flowed toward the shipyard. They had come to watch and celebrate 401's launch. Workmen received the order to stand clear. A red rocket tore into the sky. Then workers released the equipment holding 401 in place. The crowd cheered loudly as the ship slid into the water. A minute later RMS *Titanic* floated for the first time.

FACT: Along with passengers, ocean liners carried mail and cargo between the continents. *Titanic* and other British ships carried the title of RMS, short for "Royal Mail Steamer."

Titanic sank on April 15, 1912, after striking an iceberg in the North Atlantic Ocean.

The ship was not done yet. It would be nearly a year before the great ship was ready to depart on its maiden voyage. Altogether it took three years to build *Titanic*. But when disaster struck on the night of April 14, 1912, the giant ship sank in less than three hours.

Titanic launches in Harland and Wolff's Belfast shipyard in 1911.

Dreaming Up Giants

Cunard Line and White Star Line competed for passengers. They boasted about the speed and luxury of their ships.

Today jets fly passengers across the Atlantic Ocean in a matter of hours. In 1900, however, the crossing took about five days aboard passenger ships.

In Great Britain two companies dominated the transatlantic passenger ship business: Cunard Line and White Star Line.

In 1906 Cunard added two huge, fancy, and fast ocean liners to its fleet: *Lusitania* and *Mauretania*. Officials at White Star Line felt the need to match or beat Cunard.

FACT: Passenger ships of *Titanic's* era competed to cross the North Atlantic in the fastest time. Ships setting a new speed record received an unofficial honor called the Blue Riband. In 1907 *Lusitania* earned the honor. It became the first passenger ship to make the crossing in less than five days.

LUSITANIA AT A GLANCE

- COMPANY: Cunard Line
- MAIDEN VOYAGE: September 1907
- LENGTH: 787 feet (240 meters)
- CAPACITY: 3,125 passengers and crew
- TOP SPEED: 27 knots (31 miles per hour)
- FATE: Sunk by a torpedo in 1915, near the beginning of World War I (1914–1918)

MAURETANIA AT A GLANCE

- COMPANY: Cunard Line
- MAIDEN VOYAGE: November 1907
- LENGTH: 790 feet (241 m)
- CAPACITY: 2,967 passengers and crew
- TOP SPEED: 27 knots (31 mph)
- FATE: Retired and scrapped in 1934

Visionaries

As legend has it, the idea for *Titanic* took shape on a summer evening in 1907. J. Bruce Ismay joined William James Pirrie for dinner at Pirrie's London mansion.

Ismay knew the business of ocean liners. Pirrie knew how to build them. Ismay was managing director of the White Star Line. Pirrie was a partner at Harland and Wolff, one of the biggest and best shipyards in the world.

Ismay and Pirrie came up with a plan to compete with Cunard. They would build three superliners: *Olympic*, *Titanic*, and *Britannic*. The ships would not be as fast as Cunard's. However, they would be the biggest and most luxurious.

TITANIC AT A GLANCE

- COMPANY: White Star Line
- MAIDEN VOYAGE: April 1912
- LENGTH: 883 feet (269 m)
- CAPACITY: 3,547 passengers and crew
- TOP SPEED: 24 knots (28 mph)
- FATE: Sunk in April 1912

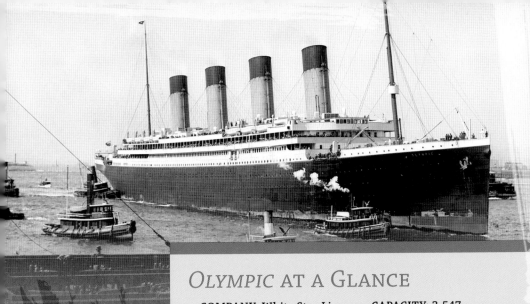

Olympic at a Glance

- COMPANY: White Star Line
- MAIDEN VOYAGE: June 1911
- LENGTH: 883 feet (269 m)
- CAPACITY: 3,547 passengers and crew
- TOP SPEED: 23 knots (26.5 mph)
- FATE: Retired in 1935

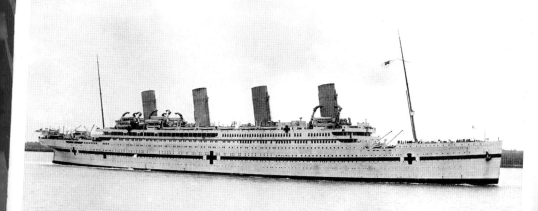

Britannic at a Glance

- COMPANY: White Star Line
- MAIDEN VOYAGE: November 1915
- LENGTH: 883 feet (269 m)
- CAPACITY: 3,547 passengers and crew
- TOP SPEED: 23 knots (26.5 mph)
- FATE: Never saw service as a passenger liner; became a hospital ship during World War I; sunk by an underwater mine in November 1916

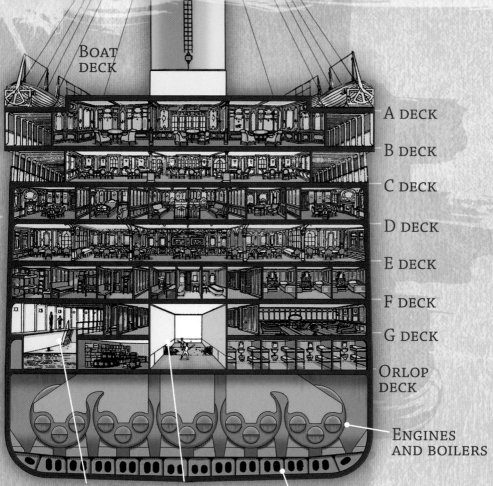

BOAT DECK

A DECK

B DECK

C DECK

D DECK

E DECK

F DECK

G DECK

ORLOP DECK

ENGINES AND BOILERS

BILGE (THE BOTTOM COMPARTMENT OF A SHIP THAT EXTENDS TO A SHIP'S SIDES)

SWIMMING POOL

SQUASH COURT

White Star Line's Olympic-class ships would combine size and speed with the features of the world's fanciest hotels.

Designing Olympics

Pirrie and Ismay's vision began to take shape on paper in the second half of 1907. Architects, engineers, and interior decorators mapped out every inch of the first two Olympic-class ships: *Olympic* and *Titanic*. Their names fit their enormous sizes. Architects and draftsmen turned sketches and ideas into detailed drawings of the ships.

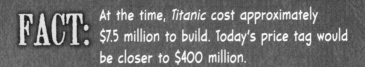

FACT: At the time, *Titanic* cost approximately $7.5 million to build. Today's price tag would be closer to $400 million.

Pirrie oversaw the technical plans—the basic structure and engines for the new ships.

WILLIAM JAMES PIRRIE

THOMAS ANDREWS

In July 1908 Harland and Wolff's designers presented the plans to Ismay and other White Star Line executives. Ismay approved the plans and signed the papers to begin construction.

Pirrie's nephew, Thomas Andrews, soon took over for Alexander Montgomery Carlisle as head of the design department for *Titanic*. Sketches became drawings, and teams of draftsmen turned those drawings into blueprints.

J. BRUCE ISMAY

Strength, Power, and Luxury

As designed, *Titanic* was almost as long as three football fields. From the base of its hull to the top of its stacks, it was as tall as a 17-story building.

The ship's rounded stern allowed it to maneuver when docking.

A fourth funnel was added for looks and ventilation.

Central propeller

Side propeller

One central propeller and twin side propellers drove the ship.

The rudder steered the ship. *Titanic's* rudder was about 78 feet (24 m) tall and 15 feet (5 m) wide.

One of *Titanic's* side propellers lies in the ship's wreckage on the ocean floor.

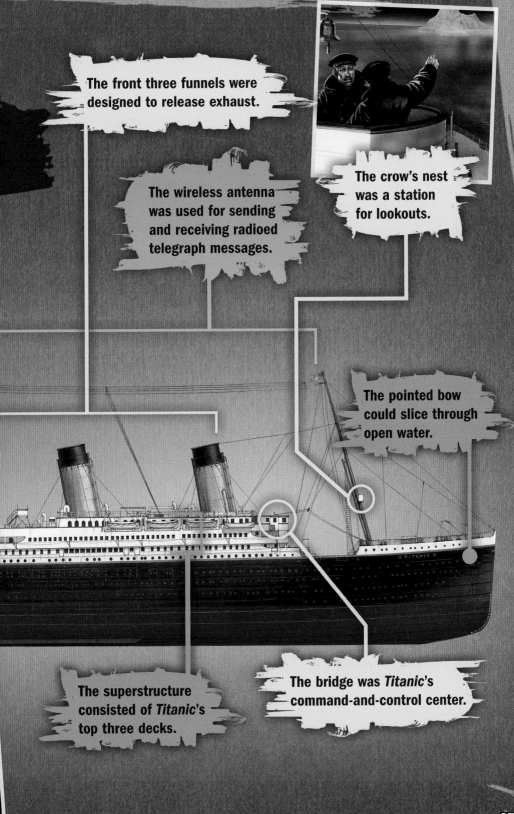

The front three funnels were designed to release exhaust.

The crow's nest was a station for lookouts.

The wireless antenna was used for sending and receiving radioed telegraph messages.

The pointed bow could slice through open water.

The superstructure consisted of *Titanic*'s top three decks.

The bridge was *Titanic*'s command-and-control center.

Double-bottom hull

Hull and Bulkheads

The record sizes of *Olympic* and *Titanic* required new construction designs. The ships needed great strength to sail the North Atlantic's rough seas. Huge waves and fearsome storms could twist a ship to pieces.

Titanic's architects designed a double bottom for the ship. The double floor of steel reinforced the hull's overall strength. The open space between the two bottoms doubled as tanks for ballast and fresh drinking water.

When *Titanic* hit the iceberg, water flooded into six of the ship's 16 compartments.

Bulkhead

Bulkheads added to the hull's strength. These steel walls divided the lower decks into 16 compartments. If the ship collided with something, watertight steel doors in the bulkheads would quickly shut. Any leak would be contained in one compartment. Designers calculated the ship could remain afloat as long as no more than three compartments flooded.

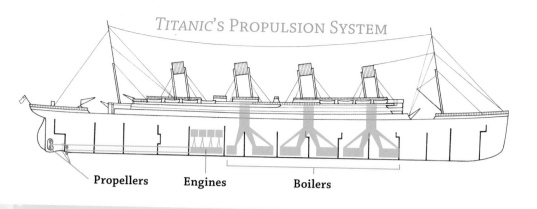

Propellers   Engines   Boilers

Power

Titanic's power came from the ship's huge engines.
They powered the ship's three propellers.

Propellers

Long shafts transferred power from the engines to
the propellers. The propellers moved the ship forward and
backward. They also helped with the ship's turning ability.

The left and right propellers were 23.5 feet (7 m)
in diameter. The central propeller was smaller,
with a diameter of 17 feet (5 m).

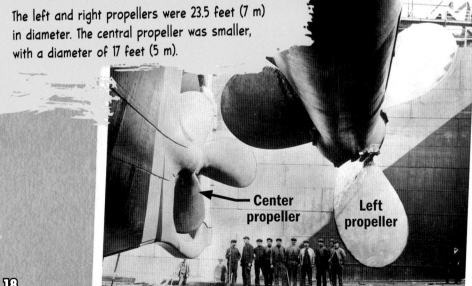

Center propeller

Left propeller

Engines

Titanic's design included three steam-powered engines. Two were piston engines that used a pumping motion. These were the largest ever built at the time. The engines drove the ship's port and starboard propellers. The third engine was a turbine. It used a spinning motion, similar to a fan. Exhaust steam from the other engines fed the turbine. It powered the central propeller.

Boilers are lined up and ready to be installed in *Olympic* and *Titanic*.

Boilers

Titanic included 29 boilers heated by 159 coal-burning furnaces. The steam they generated powered the ship's three engines. The smoky, black exhaust poured through the ship's three forward stacks.

Command and Control

The bridge serves as a ship's central control center. From there, officers command the ship's speed and course. *Titanic*'s main bridge looked down on the front deck. It contained the wheelhouse, where the steering wheel, known as the helm, was located.

This structure once held *Titanic*'s steering wheel. It is all that is left of the ship's wheelhouse.

No photographs of *Titanic*'s bridge exist, but most historians believe *Olympic*'s bridge (shown) was identical.

Titanic's officers would have ordered increases and decreases in the ship's speed using signal dials similar to this one.

For a vessel as big as *Titanic*, people needed a way to communicate between sections of the ship. Officers on the bridge and in the engine room had to signal to one another quickly and clearly. This was especially true in the event of an emergency.

Workers wired large signal dials between the bridge and the engine room. Using the dial officers could order a change in the ship's speed or direction.

ENGINE DEAD SLOW
SLOW
HALF
FULL
AHEAD
STOP
FINISH
ENGINE DEAD SLOW
SLOW
HALF
FULL
ASTERN

ENGINE ROOM TELEGRAPH

Luxury

A palace sailing across the sea—that was the vision designers had for *Titanic*. The ship's second-class accommodations were better than first-class on other ocean liners. Even third-class cabins were tastefully crafted. White Star Line officials made it clear they wanted no expense spared on *Titanic*.

★ Designers selected plush furniture, crystal light fixtures, china dishware, and fine art.

★ Ship designs included two barbershops and a gymnasium with exercise machines.

★ Exotic Turkish baths provided a spa experience where first-class passengers could steam away their cares.

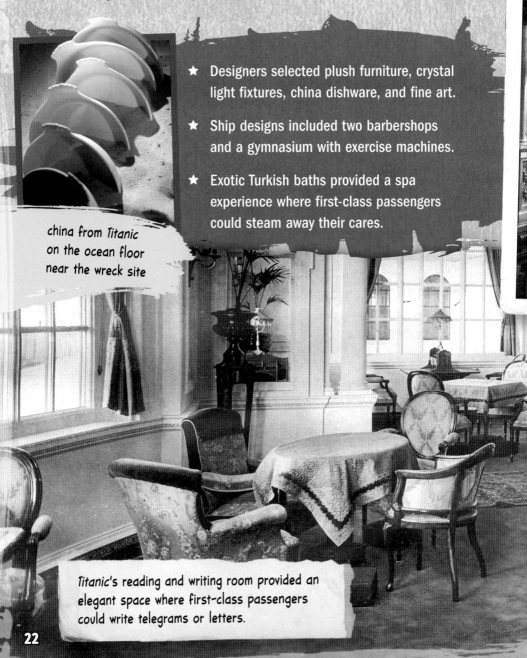

china from *Titanic* on the ocean floor near the wreck site

Titanic's reading and writing room provided an elegant space where first-class passengers could write telegrams or letters.

Titanic's Grand Staircase

★ The sweeping Grand Staircase was set beneath a glass dome in the first-class areas. It showcased the ship's grand style.

★ Four elevators were also part of the design: three for first-class passengers and one for second-class.

★ Dining saloons, cafés, and lounges served passengers in several locations.

Safety

Experts at the time believed *Olympic* and *Titanic* were both practically unsinkable because of their design. Thick steel plating, a double bottom, and sturdy bulkheads gave these ships great strength. Engineers built other safety systems into the ships too.

Pumps

Titanic's designers gave the ship eight steam-powered pumps. These pumps could take in and pump out seawater. Five pumps balanced the ship. By adjusting water levels in the double bottom, the crew could make the ship ride more smoothly. Three bilge pumps pumped out wastewater as needed. Combined, these pumps could move 1,700 tons (1,542 metric tons) of water an hour.

Lifeboats

Titanic's layout allowed it to carry as many as 64 lifeboats. That was enough to rescue every passenger and crew member on a full ship. But regulations required a ship of *Titanic's* size to carry enough lifeboats for only about 960 people. In addition Ismay did not want lifeboats cluttering up *Titanic's* deck where passengers would stroll. When *Titanic* left on its first voyage, it carried 20 lifeboats, enough for 1,178 people.

After *Titanic's* sinking, the lifeboats were all that was left floating of the great ship.

A reproduction of *Titanic*'s Marconi room can be seen at the Mystic Aquarium & Institute for Exploration in Connecticut.

Marconi Wireless

Titanic had its own Marconi room. This office housed a wireless telegraph. It was named for the inventor of that device. The wireless telegraph was new technology. It allowed ships at sea to send and receive messages and calls for help.

LIFE VESTS AND FREEZING WATER

Designers ordered more than 3,000 life vests for *Titanic*. However, these flotation devices offered no protection from the cold waters of the North Atlantic. In April water temperatures there can hover around freezing at 32 degrees Fahrenheit (0 degrees Celsius). Such cold water quickly drains heat from the body. People floating in it may pass out in less than 15 minutes. They are likely to die within 15 to 45 minutes.

a life vest from *Titanic*

From Sketches to Steel

Harland and Wolff was considered the world's finest maker of large ships. Its shipyard in Belfast, Ireland, combined new and old technology. The latest steam-powered construction equipment did the heavy lifting. Horse-drawn wagons hauled materials as they had for hundreds of years.

Slipways

Workers built the hulls of *Olympic* and *Titanic* on slipways. A slipway is a large, sloped work area. To build *Olympic* and *Titanic* at the same time, the shipyard remade three large slipways into two huge ones. Workers reinforced the slipways with more than 4 feet (1 m) of concrete. There, the giant ships would rise and take shape.

When a hull was ready for launch, workers greased the slipway. Then gravity would pull the hull down the slipway and into the River Lagan.

The shipyard upgraded its facilities to build *Titanic* (left) and *Olympic* (right) side by side.

At 240 feet (73 m) wide, 840 feet (256 m) long, and 228 feet (69 m) high, the Arrol Gantry towered above Belfast.

Arrol Gantry

A giant steel frame called the Arrol Gantry surrounded the ships. It supported huge cranes and other machinery that would be used in construction. Named for its designer, William Arrol, the frame also served as a work platform. Workers could use the gantry to access different parts of the ships as they were built from the ground up.

Cranes

On the gantry itself, workers could shift 16 moveable cranes to where they were needed. A huge central crane could lift 200 tons (181 metric tons) almost 150 feet (46 m) off the ground.

FACT: The River Lagan was dug out to be 32 feet (10 m) deeper. Otherwise the massive ships might hit bottom once they left the shipyard and steamed out to sea.

The Workers

Of the more than 15,000 workers employed at Harland and Wolff, about 3,000 worked on *Titanic*. Many jobs were dangerous. There was little for safety equipment or rules. During three years of construction, eight workers were killed and 28 severely hurt.

The men of Belfast took great pride in working on the massive ship. Most skilled workers, such as electricians, carpenters, and riveters, learned their trade as teenage apprentices. Skilled workers earned approximately £2 a week—about $250 in today's money. Unskilled laborers—those without special training—earned half that amount.

Workmen install *Titanic*'s propeller shaft. Most of the workmen who built *Titanic* worked about 50 hours a week, performing muscle-burning physical labor.

Construction Jobs on the *Titanic*

JOB	RESPONSIBILITIES
CARPENTERS/ JOINERS	These shipyard woodworkers crafted fine furniture, cabinets, railings, and other wooden details for the ship's interior.
CAULKERS	These workers were responsible for making the ship's steel plating watertight.
DOCK WORKERS	These unskilled workers moved supplies and did other jobs around the construction site.
ELECTRICIANS	These skilled tradesmen installed more than 200 miles (322 kilometers) of electrical wire inside the ship. Electricity ran through this wiring to power *Titanic's* lights and other electrical equipment.
FITTERS	These machinists prepared and modified metal parts for installation.
MOULDERS	As skilled steelworkers, moulders were responsible for customizing the hull plating.
RIVETING TEAMS	These teams were responsible for driving fasteners, called rivets, into the ship's steel plating.

❝If you had seen or known the process of extra work that went into the ship, you'd say it was impossible to sink her. ... It was a marvelous bit of work. ❞

—*Jim Thompson, caulker on* Titanic

FACT: Workers used more than 3 million steel and iron rivets to bolt *Titanic's* hull together. The rivets alone weighed about 1,200 tons (1,089 metric tons).

The Hull

Before the end of 1908, workers laid down *Olympic's* keel, the long beam that runs along the bottom of the ship. Plans on paper began to turn into iron and steel. Soon the neighboring slipway and gantry were ready. The work crews were hired. *Titanic's* construction could begin.

The first task was building *Titanic's* hull. The hull was built in several overlapping stages that took more than two years to complete.

Stage 1: Laying the Keel

Workmen laid down the *Titanic's* keel on March 31, 1909. From there, the ship's double bottom took form.

TITANIC'S KEEL

OLYMPIC'S DOUBLE-BOTTOM HULL

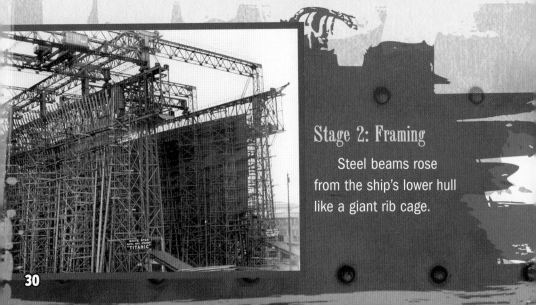

Stage 2: Framing

Steel beams rose from the ship's lower hull like a giant rib cage.

TITANIC BEING PLATED

Stage 3: Plating

OLYMPIC'S PLATING COMPLETE

Workers riveted steel plates up to 1.5 inches (4 centimeters) thick to the frame.

Stage 4: Inner Framing

Inside the ship, workmen installed steel beams to support *Titanic*'s decks.

TITANIC'S C DECK

TITANIC'S D DECK

On May 31, 1911, the 883-foot (269-m) hull slid from its birthplace into the River Lagan. From there, tugboats towed it to the fitting-out basin where construction continued.

FACT: More than 90 years later, scientists tested rivets and plating raised from the wreck of *Titanic*. Some experts now suspect low-quality iron used in the rivets may have contributed to the ship's sinking.

Fitting Out

The shipyard's fitting-out basin was a man-made lake. It was constructed on the banks of the River Lagan. Crews installed the inner mechanical workings, decking, and interiors.

The work progressed from bottom to top:

Stage 1

A crane carefully lowered each of the 29 boilers to the lowest deck. Workers assembled the engines onboard.

Deck cranes help with heavy lifting on *Olympic*.

Stage 2

Deck laying began once the boilers and engines were in place. The plumbing, electrical, and mechanical work started as well.

Stage 3

Workers constructed the lounges, dining rooms, and passenger rooms. They installed equipment in the kitchens and other service areas.

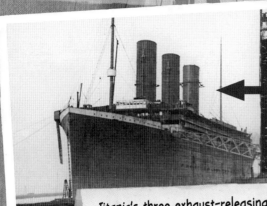

Stage 4

Workers lowered *Titanic*'s funnels and fixed them into place.

Titanic's three exhaust-releasing funnels were placed on the ship before the fourth ventilation funnel.

Stage 5

...ebruary 3, 1912, ...as towed to a .... Unlike the ...t basin, the dry ...ld be emptied. ...rkers secured the ...y pumped out the water. Workers installed the propeller shafts and propellers. Work crews applied coats of paint to the ship's exterior.

The dry dock gave workmen access to *Titanic*'s underside.

> 66 The skeleton within the scaffolding began to take shape, at the sight of which men held their breaths. It was the shape of a ship, a ship so monstrous and unthinkable that it towered there over the buildings and dwarfed the very mountains by the water. 99

—Filson Young, Irish journalist

Final Touches

With *Titanic*'s departure approaching, decorators picked up the pace of their work inside the ship. Designers wanted to impress passengers with convenience, comfort, and luxury.

Expert craftsmen built and installed cabinets and fireplaces. They added wallpaper and paneled cabin walls with fine wood. They laid down and polished wood floors. They put in carpet and tile. Plasterers and painters readied the ship's lounges, dining rooms, and hundreds of passenger cabins.

Titanic's Unique Features

★ electric heaters in some passenger cabins

★ a system of 50 telephone lines for passengers to make on-ship calls

★ running water in cabins, which was still rare in many homes at the time

★ a saltwater swimming pool

★ a clinic, including an operating room

★ a squash court

An illustration shows *Olympic*'s squash court, which was the same as *Titanic*'s. Squash is a British game played with rackets.

FACT: About 10,000 lightbulbs lit *Titanic*. Every cabin had electric lights. This was a rare convenience during *Titanic*'s time.

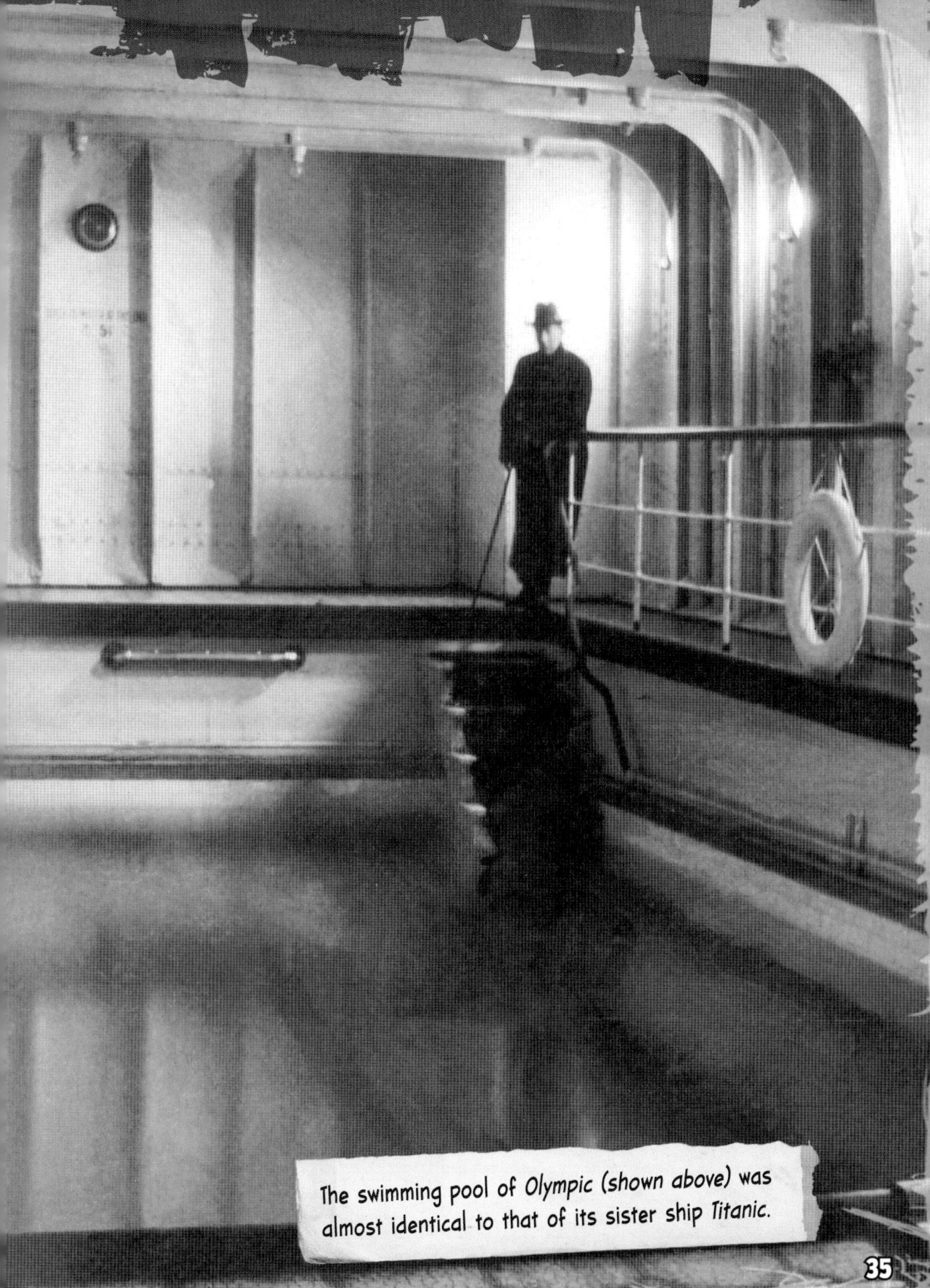

The swimming pool of *Olympic* (shown above) was almost identical to that of its sister ship *Titanic*.

Style in
Three Classes

In 1912 social classes separated most British neighborhoods and businesses. It was uncommon for rich and poor people to socialize with one another. Modes of transportation were segregated as well. *Titanic* was no exception.

Titanic's layout was designed with this class system in mind. There were separate dining rooms, cabin areas, and spaces on the top deck for the three classes of passengers.

Third Class

Most third-class cabins and common areas were located near the stern. Some cabins housed families. Single women shared group cabins near the stern. Single men shared group cabins in the bow.

Second Class

Cabins for second-class passengers were near the stern of the ship, ahead of the third-class passengers.

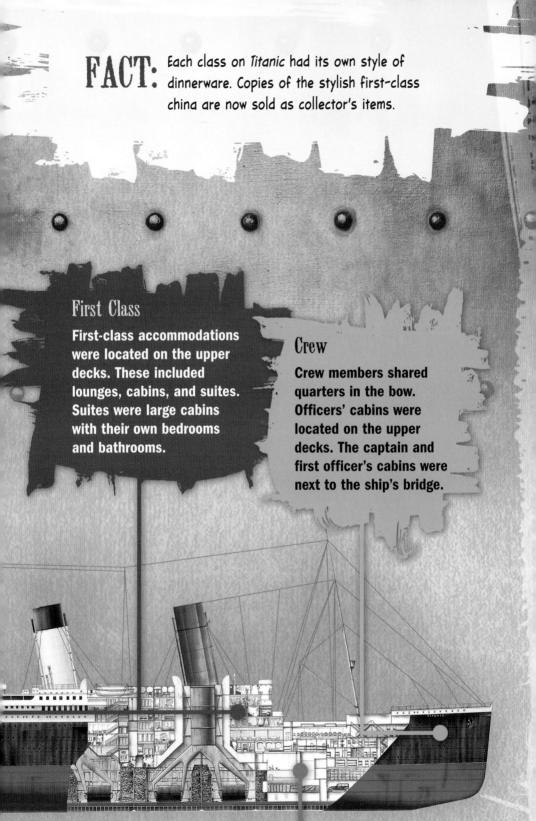

FACT: Each class on *Titanic* had its own style of dinnerware. Copies of the stylish first-class china are now sold as collector's items.

First Class

First-class accommodations were located on the upper decks. These included lounges, cabins, and suites. Suites were large cabins with their own bedrooms and bathrooms.

Crew

Crew members shared quarters in the bow. Officers' cabins were located on the upper decks. The captain and first officer's cabins were next to the ship's bridge.

Final Preparations

Sea Trials

In the early morning hours of April 2, 1912, smoke rose from *Titanic*'s funnels. Down below, crews fired up the boilers. The coal-burning furnaces turned water into steam, creating power for the engines.

The ship was about to undergo sea trials. Officials conducted these tests to make sure *Titanic* was ready to carry passengers to sea.

Titanic passed every test easily. Officials signed the papers, giving the ship permission to sail. Shortly after 8:00 p.m. on April 2, *Titanic* left Belfast for the last time.

At about 6:00 a.m., on April 2, 1912, tugboats arrived to tow Titanic to the Irish Sea, where its sea trials would take place.

Titanic Sea Trials Checklist

☑ Measure a top speed of 20 knots (23 mph), and time how long it takes for the ship to drift to a stop.

☑ Stop and restart the engines at sea.

☑ Turn using just the rudder; then turn again using the port and starboard propellers.

☑ Turn in a complete circle at high speed.

☑ Execute an emergency stop by putting the propellers in reverse.

☑ Measure a cruising speed of 18 knots (21 mph) for two hours.

☑ Drop the ship's anchors.

FACT: Titanic's anchors weighed 15 tons (14 metric tons) each. It took 20 horses to pull a wagon carrying just one anchor to the shipyard.

Departure

On the morning of April 10, 1912, Captain Edward Smith's officers reported that *Titanic* was ready to sail. Its cargo was stowed, and the crew was onboard. *Titanic's* first passengers began arriving by mid-morning. The crew guided each class aboard through its own entrance.

On April 11 the White Star Line's newest, most magnificent ship left Queenstown, Ireland, for New York. Onboard were approximately 2,200 passengers and crew. They were sailing toward an unimaginable fate. Only 712 would survive the journey. Just four days later, the ship would sink to the bottom of the North Atlantic after striking an iceberg. More than 1,500 passengers and crew members died in the tragedy.

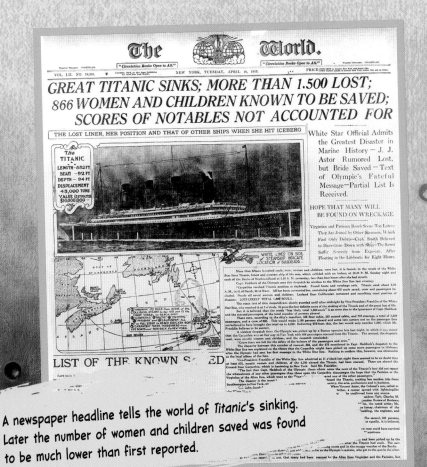

A newspaper headline tells the world of *Titanic's* sinking. Later the number of women and children saved was found to be much lower than first reported.

Titanic's Timeline

MARCH 1909–MARCH 1912
BELFAST, IRELAND: *Titanic* is built by Harland and Wolff in its shipyard.

APRIL 2, 1912
IRISH SEA: *Titanic* undergoes sea trials and passes. The ship sails to Southampton.

APRIL 10, 1912
SOUTHAMPTON, ENGLAND: *Titanic* picks up its first passengers and sets sail.

APRIL 10, 1912
CHERBOURG, FRANCE: *Titanic* picks up additional passengers.

APRIL 11, 1912
QUEENSTOWN, IRELAND: *Titanic* picks up its final passengers.

APRIL 15, 1912
NORTH ATLANTIC OCEAN: *Titanic* sinks after striking an iceberg.

APRIL 17, 1912
NEW YORK: *Titanic* is scheduled to arrive.

Belfast

Irish Sea

Queenstown

Southampton

Cherbourg

New York

Titanic sinks on April 15, 1912.

Atlantic Ocean

CHAPTER 2

Titanic's Crew

"Iceberg Right Ahead!"

I n the crow's nest of *Titanic*, lookouts Frederick Fleet and Reginald Lee braced against the cold. The ship sped through the night at 22 knots, or 25 miles (40 km), per hour. The two men peered into the darkness for any objects that might lie in *Titanic*'s path. They knew the dark water held many dangers.

As the night wore on, a slight haze came over the ocean. At 11:40 p.m. a large, black object loomed ahead. Fleet quickly rang the warning bell three times and phoned the ship's officers.

"Iceberg right ahead!" Fleet exclaimed.

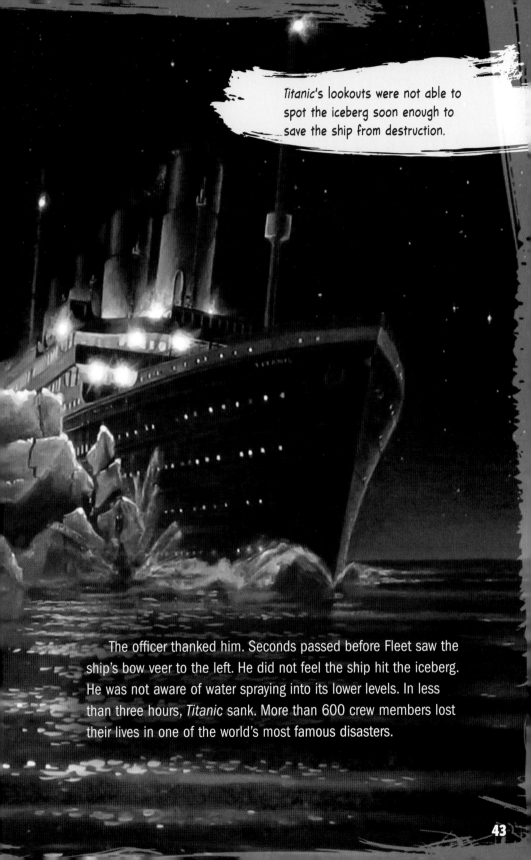

Titanic's lookouts were not able to
spot the iceberg soon enough to
save the ship from destruction.

The officer thanked him. Seconds passed before Fleet saw the
ship's bow veer to the left. He did not feel the ship hit the iceberg.
He was not aware of water spraying into its lower levels. In less
than three hours, *Titanic* sank. More than 600 crew members lost
their lives in one of the world's most famous disasters.

Assembling the Crew

Titanic was designed to be the most luxurious ship of its time.

> 66 [I felt] as many others did—proud to be selected for such a wonderful ship. 99
>
> —Sidney Daniels, third-class steward

FACT: There were 885 crew members on Titanic, plus eight musicians and five postal clerks.

Crew members loaded up the ship with the goods it would need on its journey across the Atlantic.

Crew members were eager to work on *Titanic*. When the White Star Line made jobs available, hundreds of workers quickly signed on. Most of the ship's seamen, stewards, and boiler room workers were British, but other crew members came from all over the world. Waiters and chefs were from Italy, France, and Switzerland. Some postal workers came from the United States.

When crew members boarded the ship on April 10, 1912, in Southampton, England, they expected to work hard. It would not be easy to keep the 883-foot (269-m) ship running smoothly and take care of its 1,317 passengers. However, crew members felt honored. White Star Line chose only the best crew members to be part of *Titanic*'s first journey across the Atlantic.

The Millionaire's Captain

The popular Captain Edward Smith was in charge of *Titanic*. Smith was well liked by passengers. So many rich passengers traveled aboard his ships that he was known as the Millionaire's Captain. He had worked at sea for nearly 40 years and was now Senior Master of the White Star fleet.

Smith had a reputation for keeping his ships safe. "He was a man in whom we had entire and absolute confidence," said Bruce Ismay.

A crew of seven officers worked under the captain. They made sure the ship was in good working order as the captain prepared to sail. They also made sure the ship stayed on course while at sea.

Captain Edward Smith was 62 years old when he died on the *Titanic*.

First Officer
William Murdoch

Fifth Officer
Harold Lowe

TITANIC'S OFFICERS

TITLE	NAME	AGE	YEARS AT SEA
CHIEF OFFICER	Henry Wilde	39	25
FIRST OFFICER	William Murdoch	39	25
SECOND OFFICER	Charles Herbert Lightoller	38	24
THIRD OFFICER	Herbert Pitman	34	17
FOURTH OFFICER	Joseph Boxhall	28	13
FIFTH OFFICER	Harold Lowe	28	14
SIXTH OFFICER	James Moody	24	10

On Deck

A number of crew members helped the captain and officers keep the ship running smoothly.

TITANIC'S CHAIN OF COMMAND

CAPTAIN
Commanded *Titanic*, including determining speed and setting a course

OFFICERS
Executed the captain's orders; led the ship's navigation; patrolled the ship to make sure everything was in order and working properly; kept captain up-to-date on ship's day-to-day operations

CHIEF PURSER
Took care of money and other valuables on the ship

QUARTERMASTER
Steered the ship and helped officers keep it on course; relayed orders from officers to other crew members

Second Officer Charles Herbert Lightoller

Hugh McElroy was *Titanic*'s chief purser.

BOATSWAIN
In charge of the able seamen and helped them with their duties

ABLE SEAMEN
Raised the ship's anchors and tied up the ship when in port; stowed cargo; painted, repaired, and cleaned the ship

ASSISTANT PURSER
Worked in the purser's office; waited on passengers who wanted to send a telegram, buy a ticket for the ship's swimming pool, or store valuable items

SEAMEN
Less experienced than able seamen; helped keep the ship in good repair

Captain Smith and other crew members peer over Titanic's edge as it prepares for its maiden voyage.

LUCKY TO BE LATE

Three brothers, Alfred, Bertram, and Thomas Slade, just missed getting onboard *Titanic*. They planned to work in the ship's boiler room and arrived just as the boarding platform was about to be pulled back. The officer in charge would not let them on board. Other men had filled their jobs. The brothers lost their chance to work on *Titanic*. But being late may have saved their lives. Only 22 percent of the men working in the boiler room survived.

Rounding out the Crew

Titanic's crew included a variety of workers in addition to the captain, officers, and other sailors. Stewards and stewardesses cared for passengers, while cooks and bakers prepared meals. Firemen stoked the boilers that powered the ship's engines, and engineers kept the machinery running.

Odd Jobs

Some crew members had unusual duties or job titles.

A bugle is a musical instrument similar to a trumpet.

Bugler:
Played a tune to alert passengers to mealtimes

Boots Stewards:
Polished shoes and boots

Greasers:
Oiled, cleaned, and fixed engines

Lift Operators:
Ran the ship's elevators

Buttons:
Ran errands for guests and crew members

Boots stewards may have polished shoes like these that were recovered from *Titanic*'s wreck at the bottom of the ocean.

Specific crew members operated
Titanic's three first-class elevators
and one second-class elevator.

FACT: Twenty-three female crew members worked
aboard Titanic. They included 21 stewardesses
and two restaurant cashiers.

At Sea

On the Bridge

As *Titanic* headed across the Atlantic Ocean, the captain, officers, and other sailors took their places on the bridge at the top of the ship. The quartermaster steered the ship from the wheelhouse at the back of the bridge. Crew members in the center of the bridge watched the ship's speed and direction. When it was time to speed up or slow down, they sent orders to the engine room. Officers used telephones at the back of the wheelhouse to call engineers in the engine room. They also used signal dials to communicate speed changes to the engine room. An officer moved the bridge signal dial, which caused a dial in the engine room to point to the speed the officer wanted. Behind the wheelhouse was the chart room, where officers tracked the ship's course. They posted weather reports and messages about ice there as well.

Smith and his officers ran *Titanic* from the bridge.

When crew members watched for icebergs, they looked for telltale signs such as:

Ice Blink: white light created by sunlight or moonlight reflecting off ice

White Foam: foam made by waves crashing into icebergs

Growlers: small chunks of ice that may have broken off larger icebergs

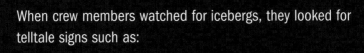

WATCHING FOR ICE

Even higher than the bridge, at the top of the ship, was the crow's nest. Two lookouts stood there on each watch. They looked for icebergs, ships, and other hazards. The lookouts on *Titanic* used only their eyes. They did not have binoculars to help them watch for icebergs. At that time, lookouts rarely used binoculars. Additionally, the crew kept *Titanic*'s binoculars in a locker. An officer who went to work on a different ship mistakenly took the key to the locker with him.

Titanic's binoculars keys

A photograph taken after the sinking shows 13 of *Titanic's* 18 surviving stewardesses.

Caring for Guests

During the voyage stewards and stewardesses worked long hours to ensure the comfort of their passengers. They carried bags, made beds, cleaned rooms, and helped serve meals. They were ready to answer any time a passenger called or rang a bell.

Although crew members worked on a beautiful ship, they did not often get the chance to enjoy the voyage. They worked up to 16 hours a day. In the evening they might have time for a walk on deck or a game of cards. They did not get a day off until the voyage ended.

A steward's white jacket was recovered from *Titanic*'s wreckage on the ocean floor.

CRAMPED QUARTERS

Up to eight stewards and stewardesses shared one room, which was often uncomfortable and lacked privacy. However, the crew's quarters on *Titanic* were better than the crew rooms on other ships. Ship designer Thomas Andrews asked for crew members' input when he designed the ship. Stewardess Violet Jessup noted her bunk was positioned in the way she had suggested, which gave her more privacy.

Feeding the Passengers

Cooks and dining room staff made sure passengers were well fed. Bakers worked through the night to bake bread for the next day. Pastry cooks and assistants made desserts. Other cooks made main courses.

In the first-class dining room, saloon stewards in dark suits took meal orders. They served meals such as lamb with mint sauce and roasted duckling with applesauce. Saloon stewards also served second- and third-class passengers.

Eating in *Titanic*'s first-class dining room was like dining in a fancy restaurant.

Titanic's Pantry

flour: 200 barrels

butter: 6,000 pounds
(2,700 kilograms)

eggs: 40,000

green peas: 2,250 pounds
(1,000 kg)

meat: 75,000 pounds
(34,000 kg)

milk: 1,500 gallons
(5,700 liters)

ice cream: 1,750 quarts
(1,700 L)

jams: 1,120 pounds (500 kg)

lemons: 16,000

lettuce: 7,000 heads

oranges: 36,000

potatoes: 40 tons
(36 metric tons)

sugar: 10,000 pounds
(4,500 kg)

Sweating in the Boiler Rooms

Trimmers, firemen, and pushers worked day and night to stoke the boilers that powered the ship's engines. The boiler rooms were brutally hot. The workers' gray flannel shirts were dripping with sweat by the time their shifts ended. Black coal dust covered the workers' faces.

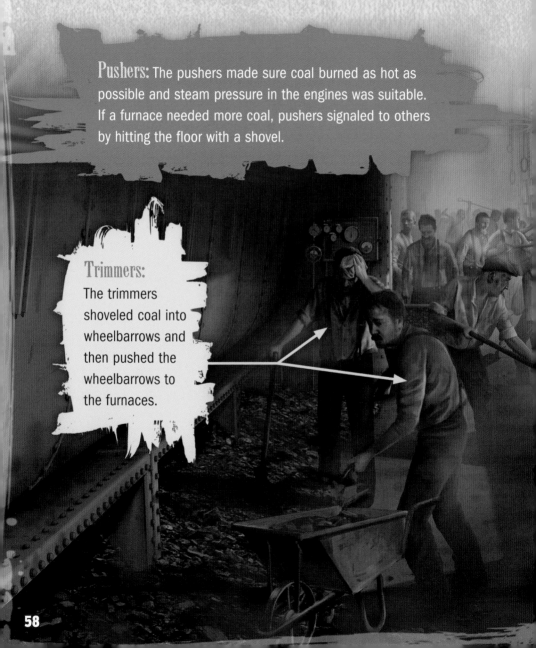

Pushers: The pushers made sure coal burned as hot as possible and steam pressure in the engines was suitable. If a furnace needed more coal, pushers signaled to others by hitting the floor with a shovel.

Trimmers: The trimmers shoveled coal into wheelbarrows and then pushed the wheelbarrows to the furnaces.

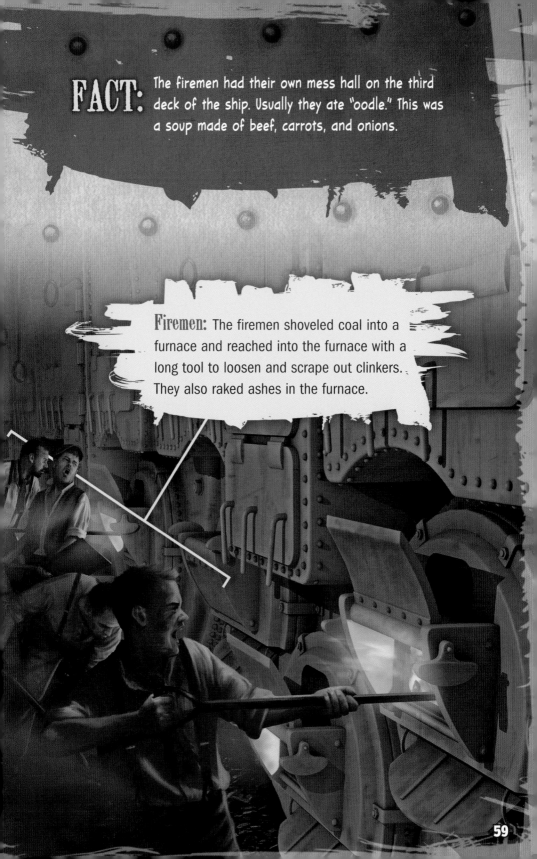

FACT: The firemen had their own mess hall on the third deck of the ship. Usually they ate "oodle." This was a soup made of beef, carrots, and onions.

Firemen: The firemen shoveled coal into a furnace and reached into the furnace with a long tool to loosen and scrape out clinkers. They also raked ashes in the furnace.

Passengers exercise on cycle racing machines in *Titanic*'s gymnasium.

MAKING MUSIC

At dinner and teatime, the ship's eight musicians entertained first-class passengers. Five of them gave concerts in a lounge after dinner. A pianist, cellist, and violinist played French melodies in a reception room outside the ship's fancy restaurants. The musicians also played during the Sunday morning church service.

FACT: The musicians did not room with other crew members. Instead, they traveled as passengers and stayed in second-class cabins.

First Class Luxury

Some people working on *Titanic* helped and entertained first-class passengers while the ship was at sea.

★ An instructor showed first-class passengers how to use the exercise equipment in the ship's gym.

★ A squash pro gave lessons on the game, which is similar to racquetball.

★ In the library a steward loaned out books.

★ Three male stewards and two female stewardesses worked in the Turkish baths, a type of spa, on the ship's lower decks. The stewards cared for first-class passengers who wanted to use the steam room, cooling room, and shampooing room.

the cooling room of *Titanic*'s Turkish baths

Mail Call

Letters and packages shipped from Great Britain and Ireland to the United States were an important part of *Titanic*'s cargo. *Titanic* was a Royal Mail Ship, which is why it was known as the RMS *Titanic*. The ship had five postal workers. Three were from the United States and two were British. The ship carried more than 7 million pieces of mail. The workers would spend the entire voyage sorting mail. They sorted more than 60,000 letters each day.

Workers in Ireland loaded mail onto *Titanic* before it headed out to sea.

This letter was written by *Titanic*'s band leader, Wallace Hartley, while onboard the ship.

On board R·M·S·"TITANIC'

Wednesday 191

My dear parents,

Just a line to say we have got away all right. It's been a bit of a rush but I am just getting a little settled. This is a fine ship & there ought to be plenty of money on her. I've missed coming home...

...it would ...ee to have ...if only for ...o, but I ...ge it.

...he band ...em very nice ...to buy some ...y washing ...post.

...service home on the Sunday morning. We are due here on the Saturday. So glad mother's foot is better. With love to all

Wallace

FACT: The postal workers were expected to give their lives to protect the mail if necessary. All five postal workers on *Titanic* worked to try to save the mail as the ship was sinking. None survived.

Staying in Touch

Radio operators Jack Phillips and Harold Bride kept the ship in touch with the outside world. They used a Marconi wireless set to send and receive messages in Morse code. An antenna on *Titanic* broadcast the messages. Other antennas on shore or on other ships picked up the messages.

Jack Phillips

The men also kept the radio equipment working. On the night of April 12, *Titanic*'s radio broke. Phillips and Bride spent that night and the next morning fixing the radio. They then got back to work sending and decoding messages. Phillips and Bride worked on the boat deck, the same deck the bridge was on.

Form No. 4.—100—17.8.10.

Deld. Date 14 APR 1912

The Marconi International Marine Communication Co., Ltd.,
WATERGATE HOUSE, YORK BUILDING

No. "O L Y M P I C"

Handed in at —TITANIC

This message has been transmitted subject to the conditions printed on the back which have been agreed to by the Sender. If the accuracy of this message be doubted, the Receiver, on paying the necessary charges, may have it repeated whenever possible. Office to Office over the Company's system, and should any error be shown the charges for such repetition will be refunded. This Form must accompany any respecting this Telegram.

To   OLYMPIC

Eleven pm NEW YORK TIME   TITANIC SENDING OUT SIGNALS OF DISTRESS ANSWERED HIS CALLS.

TITANIC REPLIES AND GIVES ME HIS POSITION 41.46 N 50 14 W AND SAYS "WE HAVE STRUCK AN ICE BERG".

After *Titanic* struck the iceberg on April 14, 1912, the ship's radio operators sent the telegraph message below to *Olympic*. The message told *Olympic*'s crew that *Titanic* had struck an iceberg and provided the sinking ship's coordinates.

MESSAGES FROM TITANIC'S PASSENGERS

"Hello Boy. Dining with you tonight in spirit, heart with you always. Best love, Girl."

"No sickness. All well."

"Fine voyage, fine ship."

Sleeping Quarters:

The two Marconi operators shared a cabin next to the rooms they worked in. When one worked, the other had a break. They worked day and night for six hours at a time.

The Marconi Room:

The radio operators sat at a workstation and wore a headset to hear the signals. They used a key to tap messages in Morse code. Messages came in through receiving equipment.

The Silent Room:

Circuits turned electrical current into radio signals. The signals were sent out through an antenna on top of the ship.

Harold Bride works in Titanic's Marconi room.

a replica of a Marconi set similar to the one Titanic used

All Hands on Deck

Warnings

Sunday, April 14, 1912, dawned bright and clear. It was a normal, busy day at sea for *Titanic*'s crew members. In the radio room, Phillips and Bride worked through a backlog of messages passengers wanted to send to shore.

The men also received messages from other ships warning of ice in the area. They delivered some of these reports to the officers, but the officers showed little concern. *Titanic* was not sailing near the reported areas of ice.

The night of April 14 was perfectly clear and calm in the North Atlantic. This made it difficult for *Titanic*'s lookouts to spot waves breaking at the bases of icebergs.

That evening, however, Phillips received another message warning of ice. It stated there was an ice field near the ship. However, Phillips did not realize the importance of the message. He did not deliver the warning to officers on the bridge.

Mesaba

ICE MESSAGES TO TITANIC

9:00 A.M.
Caronia sends a message warning of icebergs and growlers.

1:42 P.M.
Baltic warns another ship saw "icebergs and large quantities of field ice."

9:40 P.M.
Mesaba says it "saw much heavy pack ice and great number large icebergs."

10:50 P.M.
Californian notifies *Titanic* it is "stopped and surrounded by ice."

Californian

Frederick Fleet

Impact

Lookouts Frederick Fleet and Reginald Lee had icebergs on their minds when they began their shift in the crow's nest on April 14. It was a cold, calm evening, and the lack of wind made spotting an iceberg difficult.

At 11:40 p.m., Fleet saw an object in the distance. An iceberg was about 500 yards (460 m) in front of the ship. He called the bridge, and the officer immediately ordered the quartermaster to turn the ship. The officer also signaled the engine room to reverse the engines. The plan was to move the ship to the left to avoid hitting the iceberg.

However, the order came too late. The ship could not make the sharp turn. The iceberg scraped against *Titanic*, gashing its side.

FACT: Less than a minute passed between the time the lookouts spotted the iceberg and *Titanic's* collision with it.

Titanic's Journey

Titanic departed from Queenstown, Ireland, where it picked up final passengers on April 11, 1912.

Titanic struck the iceberg at 11:40 p.m. on April 14, 1912.

Titanic was scheduled to arrive in New York on April 17, 1912.

This photo was taken from *Carpathia*, the ship that rescued *Titanic*'s survivors, on April 15. Historians believe the photo shows the iceberg (*on right*) that *Titanic* struck.

Workers tried to escape one of *Titanic's* boiler rooms as it rapidly filled with water.

Trouble Down Below

People immediately felt the effect of the collision in the lower decks at the front of the ship. The mailroom began to flood as water burst in. Postal workers quickly carried mailbags to the sorting room above. Soon the mailroom was too flooded for them to go back inside.

In a flooding boiler room, firemen quickly shut down the furnaces. As leading fireman Frederick Barrett gave the order to close them down, water rushed into the room. He quickly jumped to the next boiler room as the watertight door closed behind him.

FACT: Some experts think *Titanic* would not have sunk if it had hit the iceberg head-on. The front of the ship was sturdier than the side. Therefore, if the front of the ship had hit the iceberg, it may have crumpled but not ripped open. Other historians argue the ship would have sunk anyway.

The boiler rooms and mailroom were some of the first rooms to fill with water.

Calling the Crew

On deck Captain Smith received reports of the damage and knew the ship was in danger. When the iceberg gashed the side of the ship, six of its 16 watertight compartments toward the bow began filling with water. Thomas Andrews, the ship's designer, was onboard. He informed Smith that *Titanic*'s bow could not stay afloat with that much water in it. As the bow sank lower, water would spill into the other compartments. Andrews accurately estimated the ship would sink within two hours. At 12:05 a.m. on April 15, Smith gave the order to uncover the lifeboats. When the boats were ready, he told crew members to start loading women and children into them.

Smith ordered Bride and Phillips to radio distress signals to anyone nearby. Crew members launched bright flares into the sky to attract the attention of nearby ships. The call for "all hands on deck" was passed around the ship. The boatswain, able seamen, and other crew members went on deck to help with the lifeboats. Some stewards and stewardesses went below deck to tell passengers to go to the ship's deck. Others walked around the deck instructing passengers to put on their life vests.

One of *Titanic*'s cork-filled life vests was recovered off the Canadian coast after the sinking.

Stewardesses encouraged passengers to put on their life vests and make their way to the lifeboats.

©KEN MARSHALL 1992

66 We did not think then there was anything serious. The general idea of the crew was that we were going to get the boats ready in case of emergency, and the sooner we got the job done the quicker we should get below again. 99

—able seaman Joseph Scarrott

Tragedy and Rescue

Into the Lifeboats

The engines had been shut down, and steam being released from the boilers whistled through the valves on deck. This created a noisy roar as the crew uncovered the lifeboats. It was so loud that Second Officer Charles Herbert Lightoller had to use hand signals to tell crew members to get the boats into place. The noise died down as the first boats were ready to lower into the water. Lightoller and other crew members began helping women and children enter the boats.

LIFEBOAT TYPES
Total Lifeboats: 20

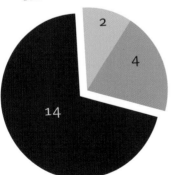

2

4

14

LIFEBOAT CAPACITIES
Total Lifeboat Capacity: 1,178

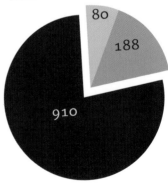

80

188

910

■ WOODEN CUTTERS
■ COLLAPSIBLE LIFEBOATS*
■ WOODEN LIFEBOATS

*Two collapsible lifeboats were not launched correctly. They were washed off the ship as it sank; about 60 people swam to these boats and were saved.

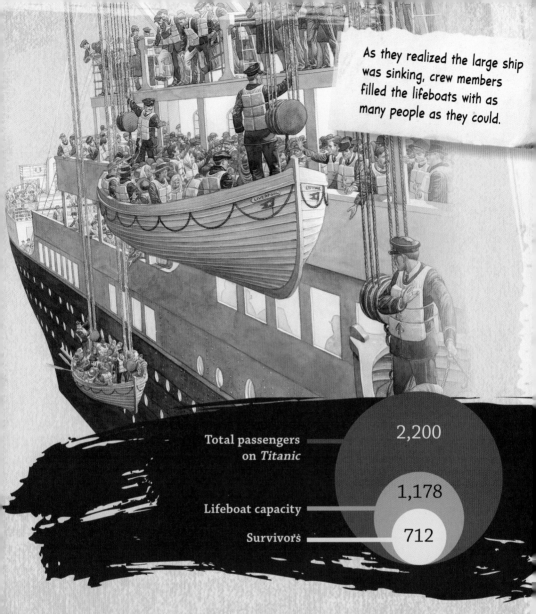

As they realized the large ship was sinking, crew members filled the lifeboats with as many people as they could.

Total passengers on *Titanic* — 2,200

Lifeboat capacity — 1,178

Survivors — 712

At first it was not easy for crew members to convince people to get into the lifeboats. They had to lower the boats 60 feet (18 m) from the deck to the water. Passengers thought it was safer to stay on the large ship. Also some crew members feared the davits holding the lifeboats would break if the boats were full. Additionally, the general confusion on deck and rush to launch the lifeboats likely prevented crew members from filling them to capacity. Investigations into the sinking suggest that more than 450 additional people may have survived if the lifeboats had been filled to capacity.

Titanic's musicians played through the panic on deck as the sinking ship began to tilt.

Working to the End

As the crew loaded the lifeboats, the ship's musicians played in an effort to keep passengers calm. At first they played in the first-class lounge. Later they moved to the lobby and boat deck. Survivors recalled the brave men playing happy music as the ship came ever closer to sinking. None of the musicians survived.

Crew members on the ship's lower levels did their best to keep *Titanic* afloat. Engineers used pumps to purge water from the ship. Firemen shut down boilers so they would not explode. In the radio room, the operators sent messages asking for help.

Officers tried to keep order as the crew filled the last lifeboats. As men worked to ready the final lifeboat, a wave washed over the deck. It swept people into the ocean as the bow disappeared under the water. A few people managed to climb aboard a collapsible lifeboat that had been washed off the deck, but hundreds of others were stranded in the icy water.

THE CAPTAIN'S LAST MINUTES

No one knows how Captain Edward Smith spent his final moments. One surviving passenger said Smith was washed overboard and then swam back to the bridge. Others said he brought a baby to a lifeboat and then swam away. It is certain, however, that he did not survive.

Titanic's engineers worked to keep the ship's lights on as long as possible.

Final Moments

Those in the lifeboats watched helplessly as *Titanic* slipped under the ocean's surface at approximately 2:20 a.m. Some crew members described the scene:

Radio operator Harold Bride said, "Smoke and sparks were rushing out of her funnels ... The ship was gradually turning on her nose—just like a duck does that goes down for a dive."

Fireman Jack Podesta recalled, "There was once when she seemed to hang in the same place for a long time, so naturally we thought the watertight doors would hold her. Then all of a sudden, she swerved and her bow went under, her stern rose up in the air. Out went her lights and the rumbling noise was terrible."

Bride survived by swimming to one of *Titanic*'s collapsible lifeboats, but his injuries were so great he had to be carried off the rescue ship *Carpathia*.

Crew members and passengers watched from Titanic's lifeboats as the great ship went down.

Second Officer Charles Herbert Lightoller said, "Lights on board the *Titanic* were still burning, and a wonderful spectacle she made ... Suddenly all lights went out and the huge bulk was left in black darkness."

Seaman George Moore remembered, "I saw the forward part of her go down, and it appeared to me as if she broke in half, and then the after part went. I can remember two explosions."

Seeking Survivors

Those in the lifeboats heard the cries of the people struggling to survive in the icy water. Most did not row back toward the survivors. Crew members and passengers were afraid of being swamped if others tried to climb aboard. However, Fifth Officer Harold Lowe and crew members in lifeboat 14 moved some of their passengers into other lifeboats. They then rowed back to pick up survivors.

Most of the people Lowe saw had died in the cold water. However, he found four people who were alive and also picked up passengers from a lifeboat that was sinking.

Many crew members remained committed to their jobs to the very end, giving their lives to save passengers and keep the ship functioning as long as possible. Of the 898 crew members who sailed on *Titanic*, 212 survived.

Only one lifeboat returned to pick up survivors in the water.

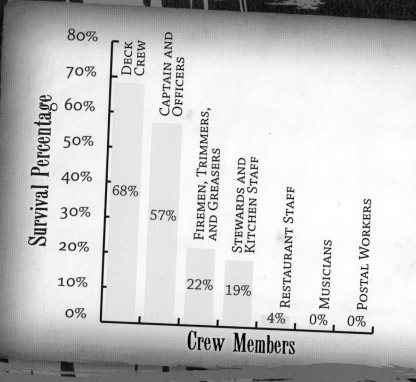

Survival Percentage — Crew Members

- Deck Crew: 68%
- Captain and Officers: 57%
- Firemen, Trimmers, and Greasers: 22%
- Stewards and Kitchen Staff: 19%
- Restaurant Staff: 4%
- Musicians: 0%
- Postal Workers: 0%

Total Crew Survival Rates: 24 percent
Total Passenger Survival Rates: 38 percent
Total Survival Rate: 32 percent

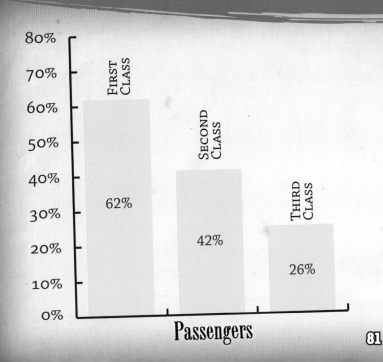

Passengers

- First Class: 62%
- Second Class: 42%
- Third Class: 26%

three stewards who survived the sinking

Returning Home

At 4:00 a.m. on April 15, *Carpathia* arrived and picked up 712 survivors. The ship had received *Titanic*'s distress call. Radio operator Harold Bride helped send the names of survivors to shore.

The ship docked in New York on April 18. Some crew members went to the hospital to be treated for exposure to the cold. Others boarded another ship. *Lapland* took 167 crew members back to England on April 20. In most cases, the crew stopped being paid when *Titanic* sank. Many went back to work on another ship as soon as they could.

The crew members who were lost were not forgotten. Many had lived in Southampton, England. Memorials built there honor the hardworking men and women who lost their lives on *Titanic*.

After *Titanic*

The *Titanic* disaster shocked the world. Committees formed in the United States and Great Britain to investigate the sinking. As a result of their investigations, several new maritime laws were passed. One called for all ships to be equipped with wireless communication devices and have an adequate number of operators. Another law formed the International Ice Patrol. This group would monitor the North Atlantic and share information about iceberg locations with ships. One of the most major changes involved lifeboat requirements. After *Titanic's* sinking, ships were required to carry enough lifeboats for everyone onboard. Stricter rules were also put in place for how the crew members were trained to operate the lifeboats.

A memorial in Southampton honors the engineers who lost their lives on *Titanic* while trying to keep the ship's pumps working as long as possible.

FACT: Sidney Daniels was the last surviving *Titanic* crew member to die. He was 18 when he worked on the ship as a steward. He jumped off the sinking ship and climbed on an upside-down lifeboat that hadn't been launched properly. He died in 1983 at age 89.

CHAPTER 3

Passengers of the *Titanic*

Traveling on *Titanic*

Titanic's passengers came from all over the world, from different social classes, and from all walks of life. Many saw traveling on *Titanic* as the trip of a lifetime.

The night the ship collided with an iceberg, all of *Titanic's* passengers faced life-or-death situations. Meet a handful of *Titanic's* passengers and follow them through that frantic night. Some managed to survive the disaster, but not all.

Jack Thayer, 17

Jack lived in Haverford, Pennsylvania. He and his parents were returning home on *Titanic* after a trip to Germany. They were traveling first class. On the night *Titanic* sank, Jack found himself stranded on the sinking ship with no more lifeboats available. How could he survive?

Ruth Becker, 12

Second-class passenger Ruth Becker was born in India to American parents who were Christian missionaries. But her brother's illness forced the family to return to the United States, where her brother could get better medical care. As *Titanic* went down, Ruth found herself separated from her family. Lifeboat space was running out. Should she look for her family or take a seat in a lifeboat while she had a chance?

Most passengers on *Titanic* believed the ship was unsinkable.

Banoura Ayoub, 14

Like most third-class passengers, Banoura was an immigrant. She was leaving Lebanon to join her uncle in Canada. She did not speak English. Banoura was traveling with three male cousins who were bound for Ohio. As *Titanic* sank, crew members were loading lifeboats with women and children only. Should Banoura stay with her cousins or seek safety without them?

Rossmore Abbott, 16

Rossmore was born in Rhode Island to an American father and a British mother. His parents separated in 1911. His mother, Rhoda, moved with him and his brother, Eugene, to Great Britain. Both Rossmore and Eugene became homesick for the United States, so Rhoda booked third-class passages for all three of them on *Titanic*. As the ship plunged into the freezing water, the Abbotts frantically looked for a chance of survival.

The Voyage

APRIL 11, 1912

Titanic picks up its final passengers in Queenstown, Ireland, and sets sail for New York.

APRIL 10, 1912

- *Titanic* picks up its first passengers in Southampton, England.
- *Titanic* picks up more passengers in Cherbourg, France.

Titanic departs Southampton, England, on April 10, 1912.

FACT: In 1912 *Titanic* was the biggest vehicle built by humans to date. It was slightly larger than its two sister ships, *Olympic* and *Britannic*.

APRIL 18, 1912

Carpathia arrives in
New York with *Titanic*'s
712 survivors.

APRIL 15, 1912

- At approximately
  2:20 a.m. *Titanic* sinks.

APRIL 14, 1912

Titanic hits an iceberg
at about 11:40 p.m.

- *Carpathia* arrives and begins picking up
  Titanic's survivors at about 4:00 a.m.

The World of 1912

Titanic was built at a time when confidence was king. Over the course of just 100 years, technology had changed the way the world worked. The world of 1812 ran on wood fires, horses, and sailing ships. But the world of 1912, *Titanic*'s world, ran on electric lights, cars, and giant steamships.

White Star Line's officials wanted *Titanic* to be the greatest steamship to ever set sail. The shipbuilding magazine *Shipbuilder* suggested *Titanic* was almost unsinkable. But in the minds of most passengers who boarded *Titanic* on April 10, 1912, it was just plain unsinkable.

White Star Line hoped to attract the wealthiest passengers to its great ship. But *Titanic* also included accommodations for passengers with less money. In 1912 much of society was divided into a system of three different social classes, an upper class, a middle class, and a lower class. Wealthy, upper-class people did not have much contact with middle-class people. Neither group had much contact with lower-class people, who were the poorest.

Classes on *Titanic*

The price of a ticket on *Titanic* reflected a person's place in society. Like all ships of the time, *Titanic* kept the social classes separated.

Millionaire John Jacob Astor and his wife, Madeleine, were two of *Titanic*'s best-known first-class passengers. Madeleine survived the sinking. Her husband did not.

First Class

Number of passengers: 324
Ticket Price: up to $4,246 (about $100,000 in today's money)

★ People in first class were often millionaires who wanted only the finest accommodations and experiences onboard the ship. Many were wealthy industrialists traveling with their families. Others were British nobility. Some of the world's richest people sailed on *Titanic*.

FAMOUS FIRST-CLASS PASSENGERS

NAME	WHO WERE THEY?	FATE
John Jacob Astor	U.S. millionaire and businessman who financed the building of several fancy New York hotels	Died
Isidor and Ida Straus	Owners of Macy's department store	Died
Dorothy Gibson	Singer and silent-film actress	Survived
Jacques Futrelle	Mystery writer	Died
Lady Lucy Duff Gordon	Well-known fashion designer	Survived

Stuart Collett was a second-class passenger on *Titanic* who was studying to become a minister. He was emigrating from London, England, to New York, where much of his family lived. Collett survived the sinking in one of the ship's lifeboats.

Second Class

Number of passengers: 284
Ticket Price: $60 (about $1,400 in today's money)
★ These people were middle class. They included teachers, clergymen, engineers, and shopkeepers. Many were experienced travelers.

Third Class

Number of passengers: 709
Ticket Price: $15–$40 (about $350–$975 in today's money)
★ Most of *Titanic*'s third-class passengers were poor. Almost all of them were emigrants sailing to the United States to start a new life. Most had never sailed on a ship before.

The Goldsmith family, Emily (*top left*), her husband, Frank (*top right*), and their son, Frankie (*bottom left*) traveled in third class aboard *Titanic*. Their youngest son, Bertie (*bottom right*), died in 1911, before the family made the journey. They were emigrating from England to Detroit, Michigan. Emily and Frankie survived the trip. Frank did not.

a replica of *Titanic's* Grand Staircase

Splendid Accommodations

Titanic's first-class section was built to be the world's fanciest hotel on water. Its centerpiece was the Grand Staircase. It was paneled in oak and included a giant skylight made of glass and wrought iron.

First-class rooms were located in the middle of the ship. This was where the boat's rocking was felt the least. All rooms were equipped with heaters, fans, and call bells for summoning stewards. Some rooms had telephones and private toilets. The rooms also had special lamps that stayed upright when seas became rough. People who had traveled first class on other ships marveled at how much more elegant *Titanic* was by comparison.

FACT: *Titanic*'s first-class telephones could only communicate with other people on the ship. A telegraph system known as Marconi wireless was used to communicate with people onshore or on other ships.

> **The boat was so luxurious, so steady, so immense, and such a marvel of a mechanism that one could not believe he was on a boat—and there the danger lay. We had smooth seas, clear, starlit nights, fresh favoring winds; nothing to mar our pleasure.**
>
> —First-class passenger Mahala Douglas

Titanic's first-class rooms, such as the one shown below, were designed to be as luxurious as the finest hotels of Europe and the United States.

Some maids were responsible for caring for the children of wealthy people.

SECOND-CLASS SERVANTS

A few servants on *Titanic* traveled in second class. Of those who did, only one survived. She was 18-year-old Amelia Brown. Brown was the family cook for Canadian businessman Hudson Allison. She was in bed when *Titanic* hit the iceberg. At first Brown refused to get out of bed to find out what happened. "I couldn't believe that it was serious," she later wrote. A second-class passenger sharing Brown's room made her get up and get into a lifeboat. That act saved her life.

Servants on *Titanic*

First-class passengers on *Titanic* enjoyed traveling in style, which required servants. In all, about 43 personal servants accompanied their wealthy employers onboard *Titanic*. About 31 of them were personal maids and valets. There also were cooks, chauffeurs, clerks, secretaries, and governesses.

Some of the wealthiest travelers had several servants with them. For instance, John Jacob Astor had three servants: a valet, a maid for his wife, and a nurse. The nurse assisted Astor's wife, who was pregnant. Maids, valets, and nurses had very demanding jobs. They were expected to handle all of their employer's needs at any time of the day or night. For that reason, most servants traveled in first class.

Servants did not have an opportunity to enjoy most of *Titanic*'s first-class luxuries, such as the swimming pool and elegant dinners. However, they did stay in first-class rooms and had access to a servants' lounge. They could also enjoy walking outdoors on the promenades.

First-class servants were allowed to stroll down the same promenade as their employers.

Second Class

The second-class rooms on *Titanic* were not as fancy as the first-class rooms. But they were so nice they would have been considered first-class rooms on any other ship. White Star Line planned to use some second-class cabins for first class if the regular first-class cabins filled to capacity.

A typical second-class room was furnished with a mahogany single bed or bunk bed and a matching wardrobe. The room also came with a comfortable sofa that could be converted into a bed. A foldaway washbasin cabinet doubled as a dresser. This provided more storage space. Unlike some first-class passengers, people in second class did not have their own toilets. They used restrooms down the hall from the cabins.

Second-class passengers ate in a private dining room. They also had access to a private promenade and a library.

a replica of a second-class cabin from *Titanic*

Second-class passengers board *Titanic*.

It is lovely on the water, except for the smell of new paint, everything is very comfortable on board.

—*Second-class passenger Marion Wright*

CANADA

UNITED STATES

PACIFIC

OCEAN

ATLANTIC

OCEAN

CUBA

MEXICO

PERU

URUGUAY

ARGENTINA

Third Class

Most of *Titanic*'s third-class rooms
held two or four passengers. But some
contained bunk beds for up to 10 passengers.
The cabins were small, and they lacked
decorations. But they were well lit and clean.
Most passengers found the cabins quite comfortable.

Titanic's third-class passengers could enjoy meals prepared
by the ship's staff in the third-class dining room. Third-class
passengers also had a large hall where people could meet, talk,
and play cards. Some third-class passengers were amateur
musicians. Evenings in the third-class part of the ship were filled
with singing and dancing.

Third-class passengers hoping for a breath of fresh air could
stroll along the ship's bridge deck, near the back of the ship.

SWEDEN
FINLAND
NORWAY
RUSSIA

2 3
10
1
9
5
4 6 8
11
7 12 13 14 18 19
15 20
16 TURKEY
17 21 LEBANON
22

JAPAN
CHINA

EGYPT
INDIA
THAILAND

AUSTRALIA

SOUTH AFRICA

1. IRELAND
2. NORTHERN IRELAND
3. SCOTLAND
4. WALES
5. ENGLAND
6. CHANNEL ISLANDS
7. FRANCE
8. BELGIUM

9. NETHERLANDS
10. DENMARK
11. GERMANY
12. SWITZERLAND
13. AUSTRIA
14. HUNGARY
15. ITALY
16. SLOVENIA
17. CROATIA
18. BOSNIA
19. YUGOSLAVIA
20. BULGARIA
21. GREECE
22. SPAIN

A replica of one of *Titanic*'s third-class cabins is shown at an exhibit in California.

FACT: *Titanic* had only two bathtubs for the more than 700 third-class passengers aboard the ship. One was for women, and the other was for men. However, many people at the time believed taking frequent baths caused respiratory illnesses. So it is possible many passengers did not mind the lack of bathtubs.

Living in Luxury

Traveling across the Atlantic Ocean took about a week. People needed activities to keep them occupied. Most forms of recreation on the ship were reserved for first-class passengers.

★ They could work out in the ship's gymnasium, which was full of exercise equipment, including cycling and rowing machines. A crew member was on hand to help passengers as needed.

★ First-class passengers could take a dip in the saltwater swimming pool.

★ A squash court was available for passengers.

★ First-class passengers looking to relax could visit *Titanic*'s Turkish baths. This spa included a steam room, a hot room, a temperate room, a cooling room, and a shampooing room.

★ In the evenings after dinner, many men headed to the first-class smoking room. There they talked or played cards while enjoying pipes or cigars.

★ First-class women often spent time in the reading and writing room, where they could read and relax or compose letters or telegrams.

FACT: Second- and third-class passengers also had access to their own smoking rooms. However, these were less elegant than the first-class smoking room.

A crew member uses the rowing machine in *Titanic*'s gymnasium.

This chandelier from *Titanic*'s smoking room was recovered from the shipwreck site on the bottom of the ocean.

Titanic's reading and writing room

R.M.S. "TITANIC".

APRIL 10, 1912.

LUNCHEON.

CONSOMMÉ JARDINIERE   HODGE PODGE
         FILLETS OF PLAICE
    BEEF STEAK & KIDNEY PIE
      ROAST SURREY CAPON

FROM THE GRILL.

   GRILLED MUTTON CHOPS
MASHED, FRIED & BAKED JACKET POTATOES

        RICE PUDDING
                        PASTRY
  APPLES MANHATTAN
         BUFFET.
                     POTTED SHRIMPS
FRESH LOBSTERS
                        SARDINES
   SOUSED HERRINGS
            ROAST BEEF
       ROUND OF SPICED BEEF
     VIRGINIA & CUMBERLAND HAM
                            BRAWN
  BOLOGNA SAUSAGE
       GALANTINE OF CHICKEN
        CORNED OX TONGUE
  LETTUCE   TOMATOES
         CHEESE.
  CHESHIRE, STILTON, GORGONZOLA, EDAM,
    CAMEMBERT, ROQUEFORT, ST. IVEL.
Iced draught Munich Lager Beer 3d. & 6d. a Tankard.

Dining in Style

Food was a huge part of the *Titanic* experience. The ship's five kitchens rivaled the finest restaurants in Paris and London. Each of the three classes had different menus.

a first-class luncheon menu from *Titanic*

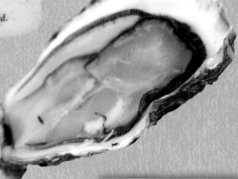

Sample of First-Class Menu Items

★ Raw oysters

★ Cream of barley soup

★ Poached Atlantic salmon with mousseline sauce

★ Lamb with mint sauce with boiled rice and green peas

★ Chocolate and vanilla éclairs

a sauce made from whipped cream and beaten eggs

a pastry that is filled with cream and topped with icing

Sample of Second-Class Menu Items

★ Consommé with tapioca

a type of flavorful soup

★ Baked haddock

a fish common in the North Atlantic

★ Plum pudding

Sample of Third-Class Menu Items

★ Rabbit pie

★ Baked potato

★ Bread and butter with rhubarb and ginger jam

Trouble for *Titanic*

an artist's rendition of *Titanic* colliding with an iceberg

> **There came what seemed to me nothing more than an extra heave of the engines and a more than usually obvious dancing motion of the mattress on which I sat. Nothing more than that.**
>
> —*Second-class passenger Lawrence Beesley, from his cabin*

> ❝ We felt a rip that gave a sort of twist to the whole room. ❞
>
> —First-class passenger Hugh Woolner, from Titanic's *first-class smoking room*

The Engines Stop

For four days passengers on *Titanic* enjoyed an uneventful journey. Then at 11:40 p.m. on April 14, 1912, the great ship scraped the side of an iceberg. Passengers felt the impact differently, depending on where they were located on the ship. Some barely felt any movement at all. But passengers did notice when crew members stopped the engines a minute later.

Once Captain Smith and Thomas Andrews determined the ship was doomed, distress messages were sent to nearby ships. Within an hour, passengers saw crew members loading people into lifeboats.

Most passengers had no idea the great ship was in danger of sinking. A few young passengers even started a game of soccer with ice that had landed on the deck when *Titanic* scraped the iceberg.

WOMEN AND CHILDREN

Captain Smith ordered his officers to load women and children into the lifeboats. But crew members followed the order differently. The officer loading boats on the starboard side allowed women and children to enter first. He allowed men onboard if no women were nearby. The officer on the port side understood the order to mean only women and children should enter the boats. As a result, many men were refused places in the boats. In some cases men were ordered off lifeboats despite the fact the boats had empty seats.

Fear and confusion filled Titanic's lifeboats as crew members frantically lowered them into the icy water.

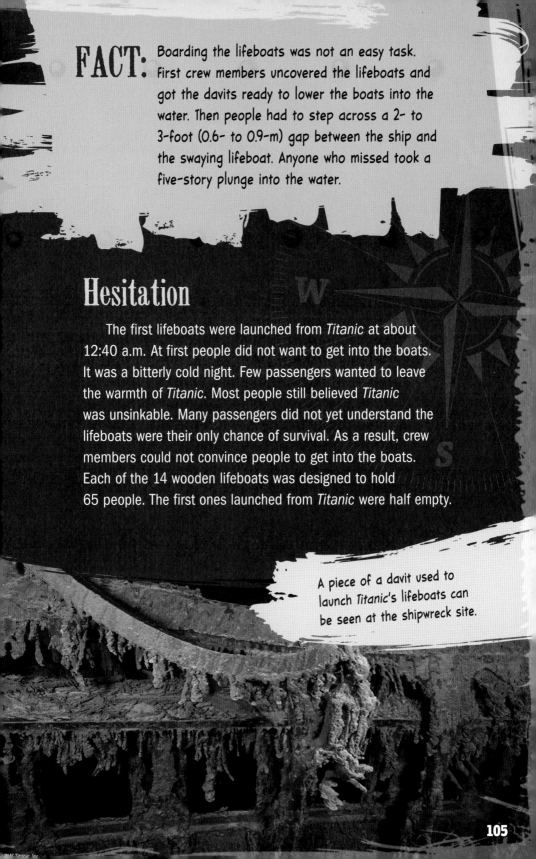

FACT: Boarding the lifeboats was not an easy task. First crew members uncovered the lifeboats and got the davits ready to lower the boats into the water. Then people had to step across a 2- to 3-foot (0.6- to 0.9-m) gap between the ship and the swaying lifeboat. Anyone who missed took a five-story plunge into the water.

Hesitation

The first lifeboats were launched from *Titanic* at about 12:40 a.m. At first people did not want to get into the boats. It was a bitterly cold night. Few passengers wanted to leave the warmth of *Titanic*. Most people still believed *Titanic* was unsinkable. Many passengers did not yet understand the lifeboats were their only chance of survival. As a result, crew members could not convince people to get into the boats. Each of the 14 wooden lifeboats was designed to hold 65 people. The first ones launched from *Titanic* were half empty.

A piece of a davit used to launch *Titanic*'s lifeboats can be seen at the shipwreck site.

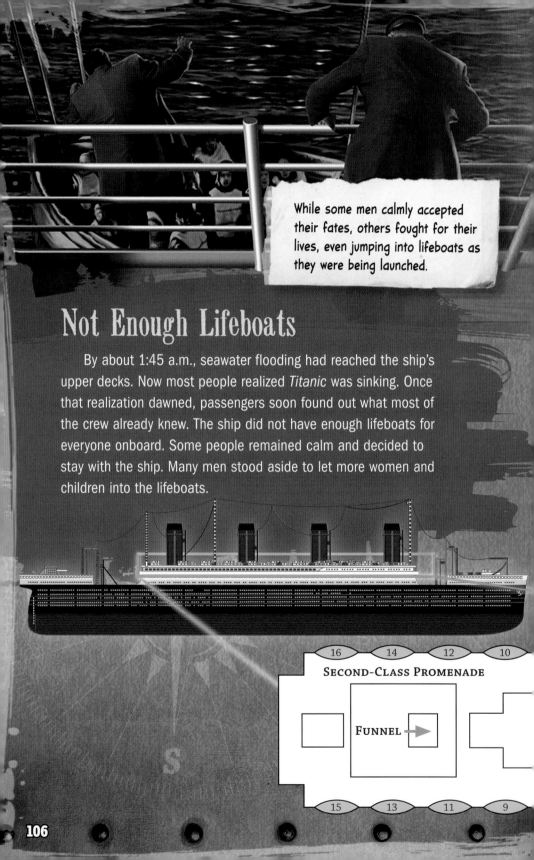

While some men calmly accepted their fates, others fought for their lives, even jumping into lifeboats as they were being launched.

Not Enough Lifeboats

By about 1:45 a.m., seawater flooding had reached the ship's upper decks. Now most people realized *Titanic* was sinking. Once that realization dawned, passengers soon found out what most of the crew already knew. The ship did not have enough lifeboats for everyone onboard. Some people remained calm and decided to stay with the ship. Many men stood aside to let more women and children into the lifeboats.

16 14 12 10

SECOND-CLASS PROMENADE

FUNNEL →

15 13 11 9

Ida Straus, the wife of Macy's department store owner Isidor Straus, had entered a lifeboat. But then she got out and decided to stay on *Titanic* with her husband. "We have been living together for many years," she told him, "and where you go, I go."

Most people, though, frantically looked for a way off *Titanic*. In some places people panicked and scrambled to get into the remaining lifeboats. People screamed and pushed to enter the few boats left.

Isidor and Ida Straus

WHY NOT MORE LIFEBOATS?

Titanic was certified to carry 3,547 people but had lifeboat capacity for only 1,178 people. However, the great ship actually had all the lifeboats required by law. Shipowners did not want more lifeboats. They cluttered the decks and left less room for promenades and other luxuries. Also many people really did think *Titanic* was unsinkable. If the huge ship started to sink, officials at White Star Line thought it would stay afloat long enough for help to arrive.

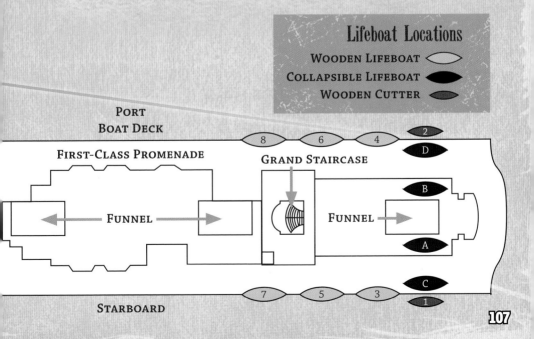

Lifeboat Locations

WOODEN LIFEBOAT ⬭
COLLAPSIBLE LIFEBOAT ⬬
WOODEN CUTTER ⬮

PORT
BOAT DECK

FIRST-CLASS PROMENADE GRAND STAIRCASE

8   6   4   2
D

FUNNEL   FUNNEL

B

A

C

7   5   3   1

STARBOARD

Lifeboat Launch Times

LIFEBOAT #	LIFEBOAT TYPE	LAUNCH TIME
7	WOODEN	12:40 A.M.
5	WOODEN	12:45 A.M.
3	WOODEN	12:55 A.M.
8	WOODEN	1:00 A.M.
1	CUTTER	1:05 A.M.
6	WOODEN	1:10 A.M.
16	WOODEN	1:20 A.M.
14	WOODEN	1:25 A.M.
9	WOODEN	1:30 A.M.
12	WOODEN	1:30 A.M.
11	WOODEN	1:35 A.M.
13	WOODEN	1:40 A.M.
15	WOODEN	1:40 A.M.
2	CUTTER	1:45 A.M.
10	WOODEN	1:50 A.M.
4	WOODEN	1:50 A.M.
C	COLLAPSIBLE	2:00 A.M.
D	COLLAPSIBLE	2:05 A.M.
A	COLLAPSIBLE	2:15 A.M.*
B	COLLAPSIBLE	2:15 A.M.*

*Collapsible lifeboats A and B were never launched properly. They washed off the deck of *Titanic* as it sank. Some people survived by swimming to the overturned lifeboats and climbing on top of or hanging on to them.

Passengers began panicking as they put on their life vests and struggled to find a way off the ship.

Panic Spreads

In second class a steward had told Ruth Becker's family the ship was in an accident but would be on its way shortly. About 20 minutes later, the steward shouted for all hands on deck. Ruth became separated from her family when she returned to their room for blankets, but she remained calm and managed to get into a lifeboat.

At first third-class passenger Banoura Ayoub remained below deck with her cousins. Some first-class passengers came down and encouraged them to leave. Once on deck Banoura said good-bye to her three male cousins and was hustled into one of *Titanic*'s collapsible lifeboats.

Third-class passenger Rossmore Abbott and his family were unable to get into a lifeboat. They tried to stay on *Titanic* as long as possible. But all three family members were swept off the deck as seawater flooded onboard. The three swam to canvas lifeboat Collapsible A. It was full of water because it had not been launched properly. The boys helped their mother into the boat. Then they held onto the sides and waited.

> **Rowing away looking at the *Titanic*, it was a beautiful sight outlined against the starry sky, every porthole and saloon blazing with light.**
>
> —*Second-class passenger Ruth Becker*

FACT: The seawater around *Titanic* was about 28 degrees Fahrenheit (minus 2 degrees Celsius). At this temperature, most people in the water would die in less than 30 minutes.

In the Water

An Icy Swim

By approximately 2:05 a.m., all but two collapsible lifeboats had been launched. Passengers still onboard *Titanic* faced limited options. The ship was sinking fast.

First-class passenger Jack Thayer became separated from his mother and father in the chaos on deck. Thayer debated what to do, finally deciding to swim for a boat. He jumped into the ice-cold water.

Gasping for breath, Thayer swam through a grim obstacle course. One of *Titanic*'s four funnels fell and landed about 10 yards (9 m) away. Thayer was freezing and exhausted by the time he reached an overturned boat. Along with 28 other soaking wet men who had climbed onto the boat, Thayer watched as *Titanic*'s rear section rose into the air. There was a massive crashing sound as the ship split in two.

Titanic split in half, and then its front section plunged toward the ocean floor.

Some of the men who survived the sinking took refuge on an overturned lifeboat.

66 **The ship then corkscrewed around so that the propeller, rudder, and all seemed to go right over the heads of us on the upturned boat. Of course the lights now were all out. The ship seemed to hang in this position for minutes. Then with a dive and final plunge, the *Titanic* went under the water with very little apparent suction or noise.** 99

—*First-class passenger Jack Thayer*

Survival

Once in the lifeboats, passengers had no choice but to wait for rescue. In their lifeboats Banoura Ayoub and Ruth Becker listened to the wails of mothers who had lost track of their children in the chaos.

The situation was more perilous for Jack Thayer and the 28 men on the overturned collapsible lifeboat B. One of the men, Harold Bride, worked as a wireless operator on *Titanic*. He told the men the ship *Carpathia* should reach them by around 4:00 a.m.

Rossmore Abbott and his brother, Eugene, clung to the edge of Collapsible A. Inside the boat, their mother, Rhoda, was too cold to speak. She watched helplessly as Eugene lost his grip and slipped into the Atlantic. Soon after, Rossmore did the same.

While *Titanic*'s survivors waited in the lifeboats, *Carpathia*'s captain, Arthur Rostron, raced his ship toward the survivors.

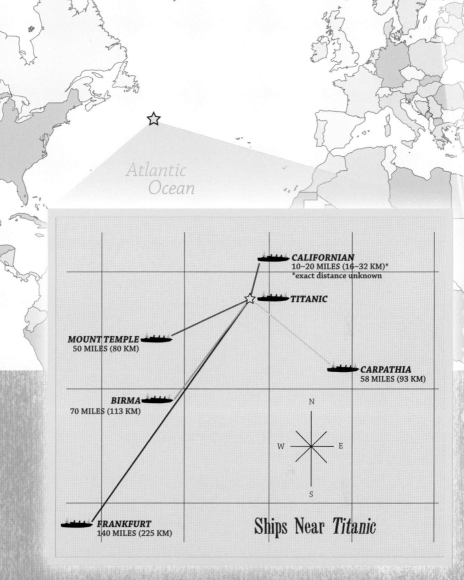

Atlantic Ocean

CALIFORNIAN
10–20 MILES (16–32 KM)*
*exact distance unknown

TITANIC

MOUNT TEMPLE
50 MILES (80 KM)

CARPATHIA
58 MILES (93 KM)

BIRMA
70 MILES (113 KM)

N
W   E
S

FRANKFURT
140 MILES (225 KM)

Ships Near *Titanic*

FACT: The ship *Californian* was within 20 miles (32 km) of *Titanic* when the great ship struck the iceberg. However, *Californian's* wireless operator had gone to bed when *Titanic's* operators sent the distress call. *Californian* did not receive the message until it was too late.

A Handful of Lifeboats

For survivors the half hour that followed the sinking was agonizing. Most of the more than 1,500 people who had not reached the lifeboats were alive in the water. But they were dying of hypothermia. They could survive no longer than a half hour in the freezing-cold water. Many died much sooner.

Titanic's life vests kept survivors afloat, but they offered no protection from the freezing water.

Frankie Goldsmith was 9 years old when he survived *Titanic*'s sinking in one of the ship's collapsible lifeboats. He later compared the cries of the people in the water to the roar of a crowd at a baseball game.

Within 15 minutes the roar had mostly died down. Soon more than 1,500 people were dead in the water.

A replica of one of *Titanic*'s wooden lifeboats can be seen in Belfast, Ireland.

STRANGE QUESTIONS AT THE TITANIC INQUIRY

one of *Titanic*'s collapsible lifeboats, loaded with passengers waiting for rescue

66 **There was nothing, just this deathly, terrible silence in the dark night with the stars overhead.** 99

—*Eva Hart, seven-year-old survivor*

FACT: *Titanic* had several four-legged and winged passengers. There were 12 dogs, as well as several cats, chickens, and pet birds. Only three small lapdogs survived the sinking.

It was bitterly cold in the lifeboats as *Titanic's* passengers awaited rescue.

French brothers Michel (*left*) and Edmond (*right*) were only 4 and 2 when they survived the *Titanic* disaster in collapsible lifeboat D. Their father died in the sinking.

Harold Lowe (*left*), shown with Officer Charles Lightoller, was the only officer to return to pull survivors from the water.

A Long, Cold Night

The lifeboats held their own terrors. Many people had no idea when, or if, help would come. Few passengers were dressed for the bitterly cold night. Many were in thin nightclothes. Some were soaking wet, or their feet and legs were covered in standing water in the bottom of the boat. People cried, argued, sang religious hymns, and prayed.

Only one lifeboat went back to search for survivors. Like many others in the lifeboats, Officer Harold Lowe feared his boat would be swamped by going back to pick up survivors. So he waited until the survivors in the water stopped shouting. It was a fatal delay. By the time the boat returned, almost everyone was dead. Lowe pulled only four people from the water after *Titanic* sank. One died shortly after being brought aboard Lowe's lifeboat.

The Aftermath

Titanic survivors on Carpathia

Rescue!

Several ships heard *Titanic*'s distress call. One of the closest was *Carpathia*. It was 58 miles (93 km) from *Titanic*, which was more than four hours away. *Carpathia*'s captain, Arthur Rostron, had immediately turned his ship to help *Titanic*.

Carpathia arrived just after 4:00 a.m. It took another four hours to get everyone from the scattered lifeboats onboard *Carpathia*. The survivors were given food, blankets, and clothes. Doctors tended to the sick and wounded. The ship's crew and passengers gave up their own beds to *Titanic* survivors.

There were some happy moments for the 712 survivors. Ruth Becker reunited with her mother, brother, and sister, who had been on a different lifeboat. But most passengers faced grief. Jack Thayer discovered his mother had survived, but his father had not. Almost everyone had a friend or loved one who died in the water.

Passengers on *Titanic*'s lifeboats are brought aboard *Carpathia*.

Heroes and Scapegoats

The news of *Titanic*'s sinking traveled quickly. People around the world were shocked and devastated by the disaster. Even before *Carpathia* reached New York on April 18, newspapers and government officials on both sides of the Atlantic began looking for heroes and scapegoats.

A London newspaper announces the *Titanic* tragedy.

Heroes

ARTHUR ROSTRON

Carpathia's captain was widely praised for racing to the scene. His ship was too late to save most of *Titanic*'s passengers and crew. But Rostron did everything in his power to help.

MARGARET BROWN

U.S. millionaire Margaret Brown became a popular figure. In the lifeboats, she helped row and keep spirits up. By the time *Carpathia* reached New York, Brown had raised almost $10,000 from first-class passengers to donate to poor survivors. She was later immortalized in a Broadway musical, *The Unsinkable Molly Brown*. But the play is mostly fictional.

Arthur Rostron

Margaret "Molly" Brown

Scapegoats

J. Bruce Ismay

The president of the White Star Line was attacked in the press as soon as he arrived in New York. People wondered why he survived when so many other men died. They blamed him for the lack of lifeboats, even though no steamships at the time had enough lifeboats.

Stanley Lord

Lord was captain of *Californian*, the ship closest to *Titanic*'s location when it sank. *Californian* was no more than 20 miles (32 km) away from *Titanic*. Lord's crew witnessed the distress rockets fired by the sinking ship. But Lord felt his ship was trapped in a field of icebergs and should not move. He did little to investigate the situation.

Quartermaster Robert Hichens

On several lifeboats there were arguments about returning to save people in the water. Perhaps the biggest argument took place in Lifeboat 6. Margaret Brown and other passengers argued they should go back. They were overruled by Hichens, the crewman in charge of the boat. "It is our lives now, not theirs," he replied.

J. Bruce Ismay

Ismay is questioned by the U.S. Senate Committee after the disaster.

Stanley Lord

Different Destinies

The people who survived *Titanic* went on to lead very different lives. Most struggled with troubling memories and the loss of loved ones. But their stories kept *Titanic*'s tale alive.

Jack Thayer became a successful banker and academic. For most of his life, he did not talk much about his time on *Titanic*. Later in life he wrote a pamphlet about his experiences in the sinking, which he printed for family and friends. Thayer died in 1945.

Like many other survivors, Ruth Becker did not talk about her experiences for decades. After she retired from her job as a teacher, she began attending *Titanic* conventions and discussing the sinking. She became a popular speaker. Becker died in 1990 at the age of 90.

Banoura Ayoub went to Canada to live with her uncle, but he refused to take her in because his son died in the sinking. Banoura married less than five months later. She raised the couple's seven children while her husband worked at automobile plants in the United States and Canada. She died in 1970.

A memorial in Washington, D.C., honors the men on *Titanic* who sacrificed themselves by allowing women and children into lifeboats.

SACRED
TO THE MEMORY OF
EVERETT EDWARD
ELLIOTT
OF THE HEROIC CREW
S.S. "TITANIC" DIED ON DUTY
APRIL 15, 1912.
AGED 24 YEARS.

EACH MAN STOOD AT HIS POST
WHILE ALL THE WEAKER ONES
WENT BY, AND SHOWED ONCE
MORE TO ALL THE WORLD
HOW ENGLISHMEN SHOULD DIE.
3.47

Many passengers from several different countries who died on *Titanic* are buried at Fairview Lawn Cemetery in Halifax, Nova Scotia.

PASSENGERS WHO SURVIVED

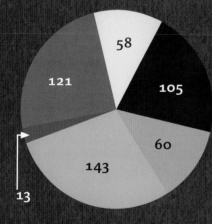

58
121
105
143
60
13

PASSENGERS LOST

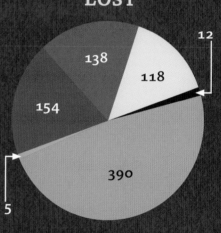

138
12
118
154
390
5

FIRST CLASS	SECOND CLASS	THIRD CLASS
WOMEN & CHILDREN	WOMEN & CHILDREN	WOMEN & CHILDREN
MEN	MEN	MEN

FIRST-CLASS DEATH RATE: 38%
SECOND-CLASS DEATH RATE: 58%
THIRD-CLASS DEATH RATE: 74%

FACT: Ruth Becker's ashes were scattered at sea over *Titanic*'s wreck.

The Last Survivors

After April 15, 1912, people around the world built memorials to *Titanic*'s victims. Many people wrote books and made movies about the disaster. But as survivors and those who lost loved ones gradually died, interest in *Titanic* faded.

Then in the late 1900s, events reignited people's curiosity about the tragedy. In 1985 oceanographer Robert Ballard discovered the ship's long-lost wreck. This prompted journalists to seek out survivors so they could retell their stories. In 1997 the blockbuster movie *Titanic* made the tragedy fresh for a new generation of people. In 2012 the 100th anniversary of the disaster also generated new interest in *Titanic*.

Millvina Dean was the last living survivor of the *Titanic* disaster. Dean was only 9 weeks old at the time of the sinking. She did not even know she had been on *Titanic* until she was 8 years old. But Dean knew her family's memories of the sinking and shared their stories. She died in 2009 at the age of 97. She and other survivors have ensured *Titanic*'s story will never be forgotten.

Millvina Dean

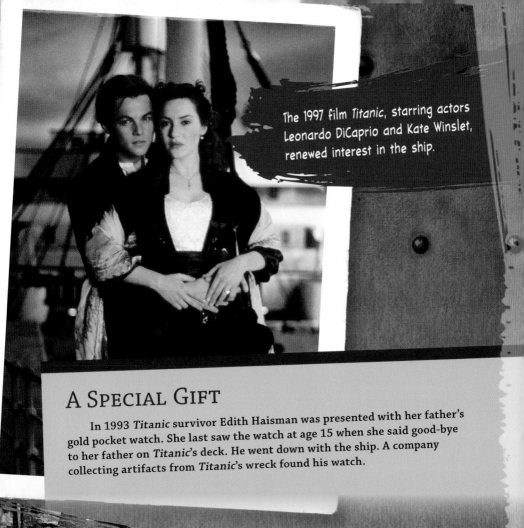

The 1997 film *Titanic*, starring actors Leonardo DiCaprio and Kate Winslet, renewed interest in the ship.

A SPECIAL GIFT

In 1993 *Titanic* survivor Edith Haisman was presented with her father's gold pocket watch. She last saw the watch at age 15 when she said good-bye to her father on *Titanic*'s deck. He went down with the ship. A company collecting artifacts from *Titanic*'s wreck found his watch.

Ballard explains a picture of *Titanic*'s upper-deck wreckage.

CHAPTER 4

The Search for Titanic

Historians, treasure hunters, and family members of victims were lured to *Titanic* ever since it sank on April 15, 1912. They wanted to find the famous ship and discover more about its doomed maiden voyage.

When *Titanic* was built, people thought it was practically unsinkable. The public was stunned when the ship sank after striking an iceberg on its very first voyage.

In 1912 *Titanic* cut an imposing silhouette as it glided through the sea.

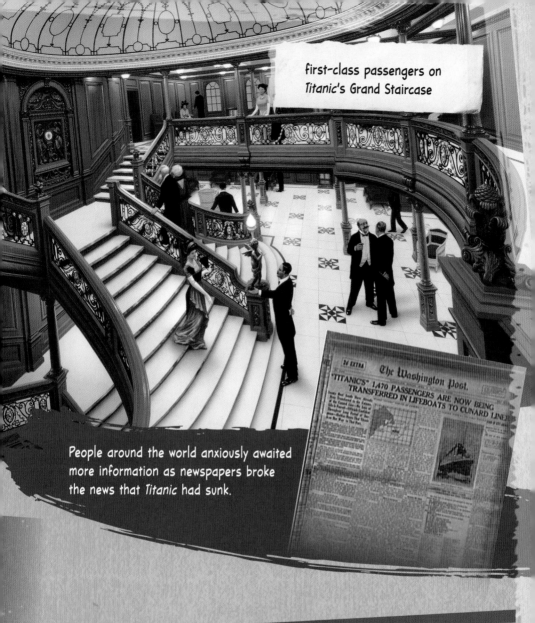

first-class passengers on *Titanic's* Grand Staircase

People around the world anxiously awaited more information as newspapers broke the news that *Titanic* had sunk.

The Washington Post.

"TITANIC'S" 1,470 PASSENGERS ARE NOW BEING TRANSFERRED IN LIFEBOATS TO CUNARD LINER

WHERE IS IT?

For years the location of *Titanic* remained a mystery. People could not find the ship. The distress signal sent by the ship's radio operators had provided an incorrect location. The officer who calculated the ship's location was off by several miles. The depth of the ship beneath the water also kept it hidden. It was on the ocean floor more than 2 miles (3 km) beneath the surface of the ocean.

Chasing *Titanic*

The first ship to search for *Titanic* was *Carpathia*. Its crew rushed to the sinking ship in an effort to save lives before the ship went under.

The night *Titanic* sank, *Carpathia* heard its distress signals. It headed toward the sinking ship and picked up more than 700 survivors who were in *Titanic*'s lifeboats. *Carpathia*'s crew did not see the ship, though. *Titanic* had sunk about two hours before rescuers arrived.

Vincent Astor was one of the first to talk about locating *Titanic*. His father, John Jacob Astor, was a wealthy man who had died in the disaster.

CANADA

NORTH ATLANTIC OCEAN

UNITED STATES

where *Titanic* sank

Raising Titanic

Soon after *Titanic* sank, people began to talk about finding the ship. Many interesting ideas were raised regarding how to bring it to the surface. Over the years people thought of using magnets, nylon balloons, wax, and even ping-pong balls to raise *Titanic*. But these ideas were never tried. People still were not sure where the ship rested.

In 1953 a British ship set off explosions in the area where *Titanic* sank. The people involved hoped the explosions' echoes would allow them to determine where the ship was located. But the results were of no help. *Titanic* remained hidden under the waves.

Carpathia picked up Titanic's 712 survivors and brought them to New York City.

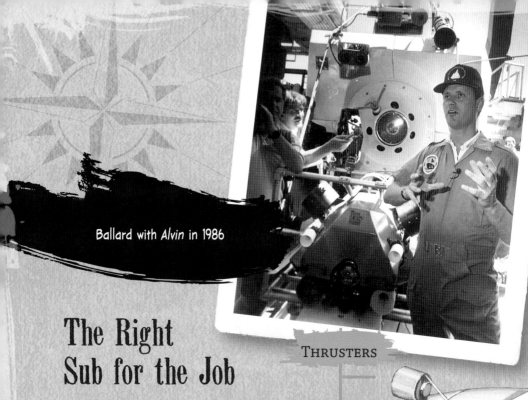

Ballard with *Alvin* in 1986

The Right Sub for the Job

THRUSTERS

Even if explorers had known where *Titanic* sank, they would have had trouble reaching it. For years explorers lacked equipment that could withstand the water pressure that far below the water's surface.

Then in 1973 equipment was developed that would make it possible to find *Titanic*. That year a tiny submarine named *Alvin* was fitted with a strong hull. The submarine could withstand intense water pressure without being crushed. It could dive more than 2 miles (3 km) under the ocean's surface. *Alvin* was strong enough to reach *Titanic* once it was located.

HULL

Oceanographer Robert Ballard was especially interested in *Alvin*'s diving ability. Ballard loved exploring the world under the sea. He dreamed of using *Alvin* to explore *Titanic*.

Alvin explores the deep ocean.

ALVIN

RADIO ANTENNA

LIGHTS AND CAMERAS

REMOTE-CONTROL ARMS

SAMPLE BASKET

CREW

VIEWPORT

Ballard's First Attempt

Before Ballard could use *Alvin* to explore *Titanic*, he had to find the ship. In 1977 he came up with a plan to use a research drill ship to try to locate *Titanic*.

Ballard and a crew sailed on *Alcoa Seaprobe* to the area near where *Titanic* had sunk. They lowered a long drill pipe through an opening in *Alcoa Seaprobe*'s hull. At the bottom of the pipe were underwater cameras and sonar equipment. The ship also towed a magnetometer. The equipment could create images of the ocean floor and locate metal objects. Ballard hoped the equipment would reveal *Titanic*'s location.

But before the equipment reached the ocean bottom, disaster struck. The drill pipe broke. It fell to the ocean floor and was never recovered.

Ballard's failure made it difficult for him to raise enough money to search for *Titanic* again. Ballard doubted he would have another chance to discover its location.

An illustration shows the *Alcoa Seaprobe* taking photographs of the USS *Monitor*, a ship that sank during the Civil War (1861–1865).

a sonar image of the sunken ship, the USS *Monitor*

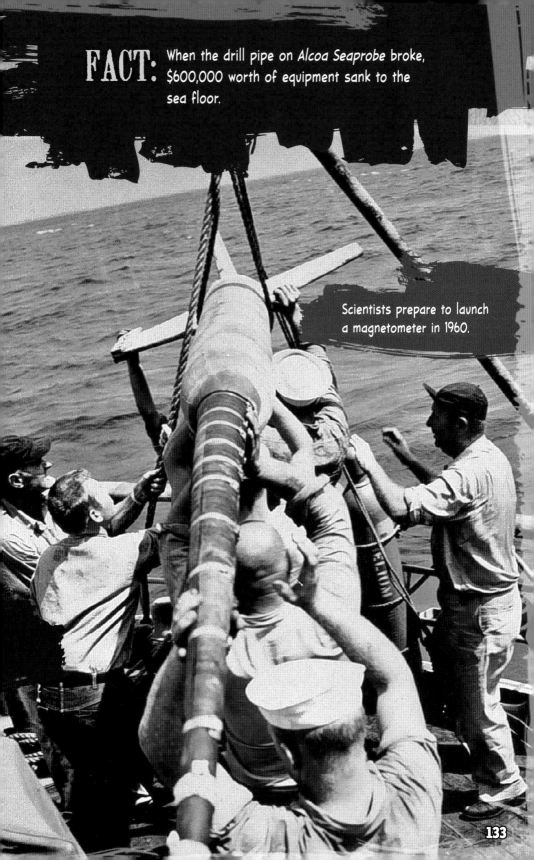

FACT: When the drill pipe on *Alcoa Seaprobe* broke, $600,000 worth of equipment sank to the sea floor.

Scientists prepare to launch a magnetometer in 1960.

Jack Grimm's Three Strikes

After Ballard's failure, another explorer decided to try his luck in finding *Titanic*. Jack Grimm was a millionaire who loved adventure. He became Ballard's main rival in the hunt for *Titanic*.

Grimm's *Titanic* Timeline

1980

Grimm and two scientists sail to the area where *Titanic* sank. Using sonar, they find several targets that might be *Titanic*. However, bad weather and equipment troubles force them to give up the search.

1981

Grimm and his crew use another type of sonar to get a clearer look at 14 targets they think could be *Titanic*. But a magnetometer shows that none of the targets are the ship. At the end of the trip, Grimm's team lowers a video camera into the ocean. It shows a blurry object Grimm thinks is *Titanic*'s propeller. The scientists working with Grimm are unsure. They believe the image is too blurry to say for sure what the object is.

1983

Grimm and his crew return to the propeller site, hoping to prove the object Grimm believes to be a propeller was attached to *Titanic*. But the sonar does not show any objects large enough to be *Titanic*. High winds keep them from searching other areas. The crew returns empty handed, and Grimm's quest for *Titanic* comes to an end.

Jack Grimm (*left*) and his expedition team display a chart showing their 1981 *Titanic* search.

FACT: Grimm's other expeditions included searches for legendary creatures and artifacts, including the Loch Ness monster, Bigfoot, and Noah's Ark.

Ballard Sees His Chance

Grimm's failure meant Ballard could still realize his dream of finding *Titanic*. Ballard also saw how new underwater robots, known as remotely operated underwater vehicles (ROVs), could help him overcome some of the problems with searching for the ship.

The Problems:

- *Titanic* was more than 2 miles (3 km) beneath the ocean's surface. Water pressure at that depth could crush equipment and make it dangerous for explorers.

- There is little natural light beyond 650 feet (198 m) below sea level.

- It was costly to look for the ship, so scientists had to cover as much ground as they could in a short amount of time.

The ROV *Hercules* uses lights to show the deep ocean floor.

Operators on a ship control an ROV in the Gulf of Mexico.

The Solution:

- ROVs could be operated by scientists on the surface. This was less dangerous than putting a scientist in a submarine.

- ROVs could stay underwater for days and withstand high water pressure.

- The ROVs carried lights that made underwater objects visible and used special cameras to take pictures.

- Robotic arms could set up scientific equipment and collect samples. However, Ballard did not plan on removing any objects from the *Titanic* wreck, so he would use a robotic arm to carry a camera.

- The ROVs could send a video feed to the surface right away, helping searchers cover a larger area in less time. If they didn't see anything of importance, they could move on to a different area.

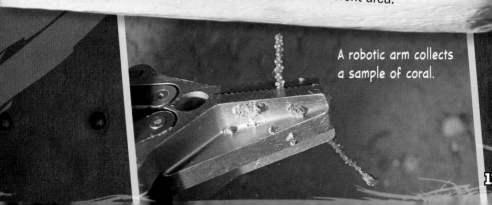

A robotic arm collects a sample of coral.

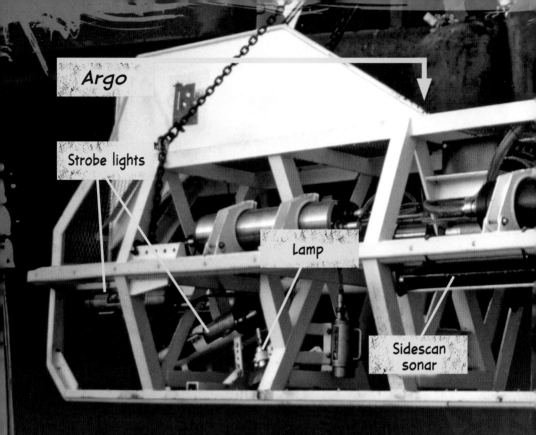

Argo

Strobe lights

Lamp

Sidescan sonar

15 feet (4.6 m) long

Weight: 4,000 pounds (1,800 kg)

Argo

In 1983 Ballard worked with a team at the Woods Hole Oceanographic Institution in Massachusetts. Together they developed a new ROV called *Argo*.

Scientists could lower *Argo* more than 1 mile (2 km) under the ocean's surface. They used a long cable to attach *Argo* to a ship and tow it 50 to 100 feet (15 to 30 m) above the bottom of the ocean. The ROV acted as underwater eyes for scientists on the surface. Its video cameras sent live images through a cable. One camera could zoom in on objects for a closer look.

Argo's lights made objects visible in the darkness of the deep ocean. In addition, its cameras made light seem 10,000 times brighter. *Argo* also had side and front sonars to create images of a large area.

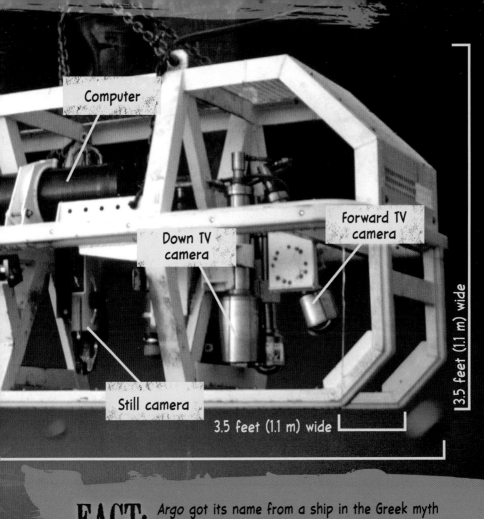

Computer

Down TV camera

Forward TV camera

Still camera

3.5 feet (1.1 m) wide

3.5 feet (1.1 m) wide

FACT: Argo got its name from a ship in the Greek myth of Jason and the Golden Fleece. In the myth the Greek hero Jason sails on *Argo* while he looks for the Golden Fleece.

Argo hunts for *Titanic* in 1985.

Jason Jr.

Once researchers found *Titanic*, *Argo* would be too large to get inside the sunken ship. Scientists needed a smaller robot for this job. Ballard worked with the Woods Hole Oceanographic Institution to create the perfect robot for this task.

Jason Jr.'s small size made it ideal for exploring the tight spaces of shipwrecks.

What Jason Jr. Was

The robot *Jason Jr.* was also called *JJ*. *JJ* was perfectly suited to fit inside *Titanic*. *JJ* looked a bit like a lawn mower with no handle. It had lights, cameras, and motors. It was small enough to be carried on the front of the submarine *Alvin*.

How JJ Worked

Scientists used a cable to attach *JJ* to *Alvin*. A pilot inside the submarine sent signals through the cable to control *JJ*. Thrusters propelled the small robot forward, up, and to the side. Using these movements, *JJ* could swim inside *Titanic*.

What JJ Did

Once inside *Titanic*, *JJ* could take pictures with its video camera and still camera. The images were recorded so others could see them as well.

JJ explores *Titanic's* hull in 1986.

NAME	ALVIN	ANGUS
DECADE BUILT	1960s	1970s
PEOPLE COULD RIDE IN IT	Yes	No
CONTROLLED WITH A CABLE	No	Yes
TOWED BY A SHIP	No	Yes
COULD FIT INTO SMALL SPACES	No	No
PROPELLED BY THRUSTERS	Yes	No
MAXIMUM DIVING DEPTH	14,800 feet (4,500 m)	20,000 feet (6,100 m)

Old and Reliable

Not all of the equipment Ballard would use on the *Titanic* search mission was new. He saw that an older piece of equipment called *ANGUS* could also be useful.

Scientists built *ANGUS* in the 1970s. They called it a sled because it carried three cameras in a 12-foot (4-m) frame. *ANGUS* could hang from a ship by a thick wire. Its cameras pointed downward and together they could take photos of an area 200 feet (60 m) wide.

ANGUS was built to work in rough seas. Its steel frame kept its cameras from being damaged if the sled hit a rock. The tough piece of equipment would be especially useful if seas were too rough for the ROVs.

ARGO	JASON JR.
1980s	1980s
No	No
Yes	Yes
Yes	No
No	Yes
No	Yes
20,000 feet (6,100 m)	21,400 feet (6,500 m)

ANGUS hung in the water on a thick wire and was towed by a ship.

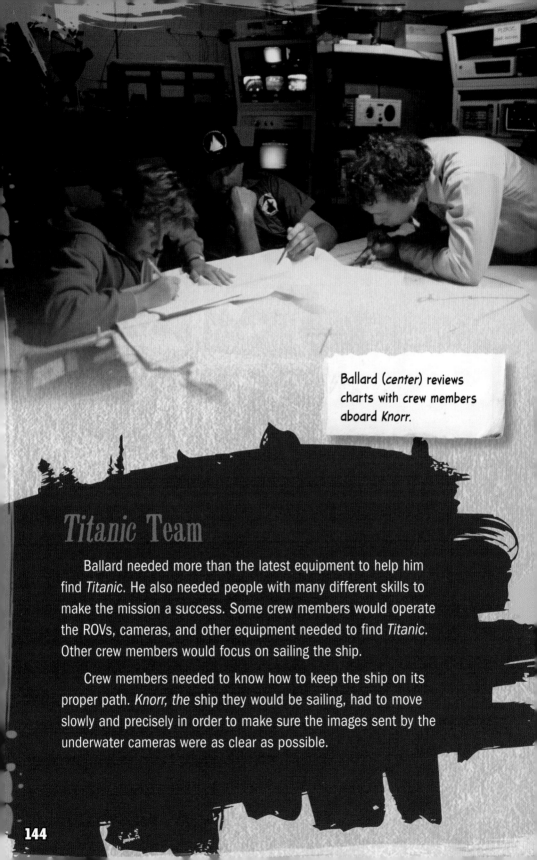

Ballard (*center*) reviews charts with crew members aboard *Knorr*.

Titanic Team

Ballard needed more than the latest equipment to help him find *Titanic*. He also needed people with many different skills to make the mission a success. Some crew members would operate the ROVs, cameras, and other equipment needed to find *Titanic*. Other crew members would focus on sailing the ship.

Crew members needed to know how to keep the ship on its proper path. *Knorr, the* ship they would be sailing, had to move slowly and precisely in order to make sure the images sent by the underwater cameras were as clear as possible.

The Search Squad

Ballard's team was split into three different groups called watches. Each watch would work four hours in the morning and four at night:

FLYERS

Earl Young, Martin Bowen, and Emile Bergeron controlled a cable attached to *Argo*. The robot took pictures of the bottom of the ocean.

NAVIGATORS

Steve Gegg, Tom Crook, and Cathy Offinger tracked the location of the *Knorr* and *Argo*.

DRIVERS

Watch leaders Jean-Louis Michel, Jean Jarry, and Bernard Pillaud steered *Knorr* and controlled its speed.

ENGINEERS

Stu Harris, Tom Dettweiler, and Bob Squires fixed problems with *Argo*.

SONAR OPERATORS

George Rey, Terry Snyder, and Jim Saint identified images on *Argo*'s sonar screen.

DOCUMENTATION TEAM

Bill Lange, Emory Kristof, and Ralph White logged the details of the search.

DATA LOGGERS

Sharon Callahan, Georgina Baker, and Lisa Schwartz mapped the search area.

Other Crew Members

CAPTAIN

Richard Bowen supervised the ship's operations and crew.

ROBOTIC RESEARCHER

Dana Yoerger worked on tracking software for *Argo*.

Ballard acted as the chief scientist, overseeing the mission.

International Assistance

Ballard knew it would take time to do a thorough search for *Titanic*. However, he and his crew would only have time to spend a few weeks in the area where the ship sank. Ballard thought it would most likely take more than a few weeks to find the ship. He needed help. He flew to Paris, France, and asked a group of French scientists to assist with his search.

Ballard had worked with French researcher Jean-Louis Michel in the past. In the 1970s they had studied a ridge under the Atlantic Ocean together. Now Michel and scientists from the French Research Institute for Exploitation of the Sea were happy to help Ballard search for *Titanic*. The French scientists wanted to test their new sonar technology. The fame and mystery surrounding *Titanic* also lured them.

The French crew had a new sonar scanner to search the ocean floor. This tool would help them find targets that could be *Titanic*. Ballard's team would visit later and send down a robot to take a closer look at any targets of interest. Working together French and American teams could conduct a better search than if each group worked alone.

The French team prepares to launch its sonar equipment from its research ship, *Le Suroit*.

Discovery!

Mapping a Search Area

Now that he had the right equipment and team for the *Titanic* search, Ballard had to zero in on a search area. When deciding where to look, Ballard and the leaders of the French team considered the location given by *Titanic*'s crew the night the ship sank. They read information about ice provided by other ships in the area that night.

The team also looked at the place *Carpathia* had found the lifeboats and how the ocean's current could have carried them away from the ship. They determined the ship was east of the position reported by its crew. The team mapped a main search area covering 115 square miles (298 square km).

As *Titanic* sank, its radio operators frantically sent out distress signals, which were picked up by *Carpathia*'s operator (*right*). However, the coordinates *Titanic*'s crew provided were incorrect. Luckily *Carpathia* found the survivors anyway.

FACT: Ballard's search area was almost twice the size of Washington, D.C.

WHAT COULD GO WRONG?

Although he had a solid search plan and the latest equipment, Ballard knew it was possible his team might not locate *Titanic*. Potential problems included:

- **Mud:** The ship might be hidden beneath an underwater mud slide that had occurred during an earthquake in 1929.

- **Canyons:** The ship may have fallen into a deep underwater canyon.

- **Breakage:** *Titanic* may have broken apart into small pieces.

- **Shadows:** The ship might be behind an underwater ridge, preventing it from being viewed with sonar.

- **Weather:** High waves could make it difficult for the sonar to work properly.

- **Time:** The team's equipment was needed for other projects. The group had only about five weeks to use it.

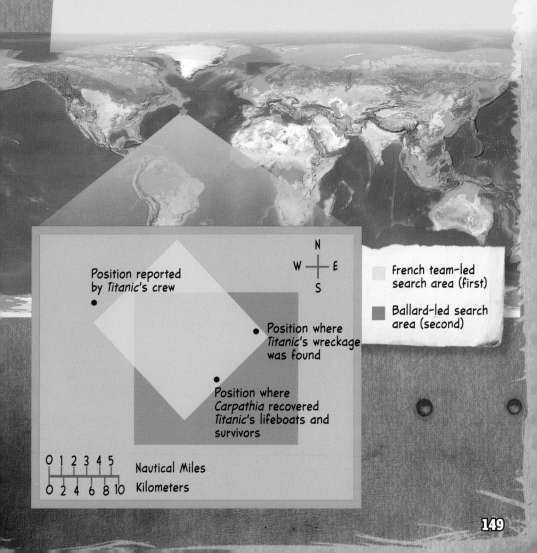

Position reported by *Titanic's* crew

Position where *Titanic's* wreckage was found

Position where *Carpathia* recovered *Titanic's* lifeboats and survivors

N
W — E
S

French team-led search area (first)

Ballard-led search area (second)

0 1 2 3 4 5 Nautical Miles

0 2 4 6 8 10 Kilometers

Scanning Struggles

The French team's *Titanic* search began on July 5, 1985. They lowered their sonar into the water and began traveling in a pattern that looked like they were mowing the lawn over the ocean bottom.

For approximately four weeks, the French crew scanned the bottom of the ocean. Bad weather kept them from covering as much ground as they wanted to. They did not find *Titanic*. However, their work allowed Ballard to rule out most of this area when he began his part of the search.

❝ By following the crumbs, we would find *Titanic*. ❞

—Robert Ballard

debris from *Titanic*

A ceramic bowl and other *Titanic* debris lie scattered on the ocean floor near where the ship went down.

Zeroing in on Debris

After the French team failed to find *Titanic*, it was Ballard's turn to search for the ship. Many people believed *Titanic* sank in one piece. But Ballard thought the ship split into two parts as it sank. A survivor who was near the ship when it went down described how it broke apart. Ballard thought this description was correct. Rather than look for the ship itself, he would look for its debris. It was likely that a long trail of items spilled out of the ship as it sank. Finding this trail would lead Ballard to *Titanic*. The debris that fell from *Titanic* would cover a large area. Ballard thought it would be easier to find the debris field than the ship itself.

SECRET MISSIONS

Ballard was very hopeful the debris would lead him to *Titanic*. He had used this same tactic to study wreckage from two sunken submarines in the early 1980s. These missions for the U.S. Navy were kept secret. Ballard could not talk about them until years later. On these missions Ballard noticed items from the submarines did not sink in a single clump. Heavier objects sank first. Lighter ones drifted on the current before falling to the bottom of the ocean. This trail of debris formed a pattern that led Ballard to the main wreckage of the submarines.

Ballard (*standing*) and other members of the team study monitors showing images of the ocean floor.

Trouble and Tension

Ballard and his crew began their search in an area about 350 miles (563 km) off the coast of Newfoundland, Canada, on August 25, 1985. *Argo*'s cameras captured images of the sea floor. All day and night crew members took turns watching the monitors, looking for man-made objects. *Argo* gave them a good view of the ocean bottom, but all they saw was mud and sand.

KNORR

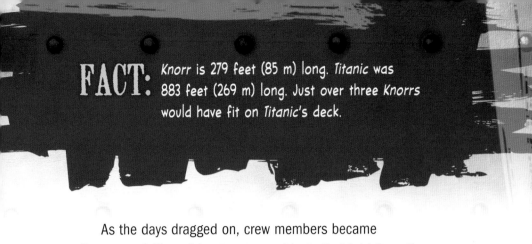

As the days dragged on, crew members became discouraged. They did not see any objects that told them they were near *Titanic*. They began to lose hope as they neared the edge of their search area.

By August 31 even Ballard was worried. A storm was on its way that would rock the ship and make it difficult to hold *Argo* steady. The crew had only five days before they had to return to port in Massachusetts. Ballard feared the mission would end in failure.

Knorr was built to help scientists study the world's oceans.

Titanic Sighting

Ballard went to his cabin shortly after midnight on September 1, 1985. He was tired and discouraged. Then the cook stopped by and told him the crew wanted to see him.

Ballard hurried to the control room. The crew replayed the tape of what they had just seen on the monitors. Ballard watched as pieces of wreckage appeared on the screen and then a boiler, which the crew had identified as one from *Titanic*. Then *Titanic*'s portholes and a piece of railing came into view. Ballard was so excited, he could barely speak. Then the entire room erupted in joyful celebration.

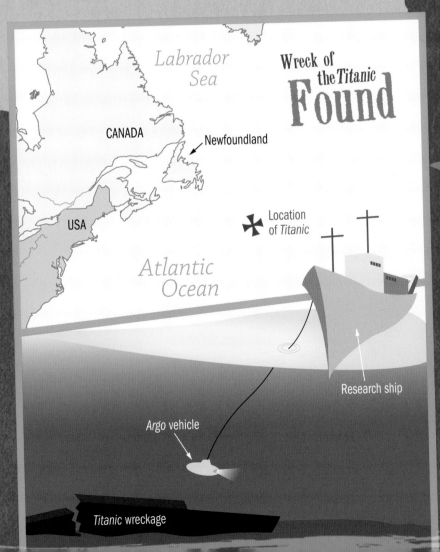

Labrador Sea

Wreck of the Titanic Found

CANADA

← Newfoundland

USA

✠ Location of *Titanic*

Atlantic Ocean

Research ship

Argo vehicle

Titanic wreckage

Titanic's
upright bow

Dishes from *Titanic*'s kitchen lie
half-buried in mud near the wreck.

Over the next few days, *Argo* and *ANGUS* took video and photos
of *Titanic*'s wreck. Ballard learned several things:

★ *Titanic* was upright.

★ The crow's nest was lying on the deck.

★ Coal, dishes, and bottles were in the debris field.

★ The stern was lying apart from the rest of the ship.

Ballard wanted to learn more about the ship's remains, but
he was out of time for his mission. The equipment and crew
were needed for other projects, and they had to return to port.
Ballard's *Titanic* mission would have to be continued.

A Closer Look

Ballard was not done exploring *Titanic*. In July 1986 he began another mission to learn more about the sunken luxury liner. This time *Alvin* and *JJ* gave him a firsthand look.

JJ's Journey

After a 2.5-hour descent, *Alvin*'s pilot set the submarine on *Titanic*'s deck. Now it was time for *JJ* to go to work. While attached to *Alvin* with a cable, *JJ* made its way in through an opening in the ship's deck. The robot traveled down the Grand Staircase and took video images. Ballard saw the beautiful wood that had once been inside the ship was gone. Tiny creatures known as wood-boring mollusks had eaten it. However, a pillar and fancy light fixtures remained.

Ballard spent almost two weeks using *Alvin* and *JJ* to gather video of the sunken ship. He saw the remains of the captain's cabin. In the debris field near the ship, he saw plates, sinks, bathtubs, doorknobs, windows, and a safe. On one of his last dives in *Alvin* Ballard left a plaque on the ship's stern. It honored the victims of the disaster. He hoped others would allow the ship to rest as a memorial to those who died.

Rusticles hang off the side of *Titanic*.

Undersea Attraction

Ballard hoped people would leave *Titanic* undisturbed. Others, however, were drawn to the site to take photos, study the ship, and gather artifacts.

A company called RMS Titanic, Inc., visited *Titanic* in 1987. The group recovered a bell, a compass, dishes, a porthole, and more than 1,000 other items from the ship's debris field. Its explorers later returned to the site to gather items for museum displays. In the first 25 years after *Titanic*'s discovery, RMS Titanic, Inc., recovered more than 5,500 items from the area around the ship. Some of the items recovered from the ship's debris field were ordinary, such as keys and dishes. Others were valuable objects, including jewelry that had belonged to wealthy passengers.

Recovered from *Titanic*

a third-class passenger's vest, which was found in a suitcase

a statue from the ship's Grand Staircase

The Fate of *Titanic*

Controversy swirls over how to treat *Titanic*'s remains. Some fear visitors will damage the ship. Others want to carefully visit the ship to study it. Artifacts from *Titanic* are very valuable. They are also very fragile. Without careful preservation, they can decay. When RMS Titanic, Inc., brings artifacts to the surface, it preserves and records each object. The most fragile objects are kept in storage, where they can be protected from further decay. Many objects are sturdy enough for travel. These artifacts are exhibited in museums around the world, where they are seen by millions. *Titanic* may rest in darkness miles under the ocean, but it continues to fascinate people around the world.

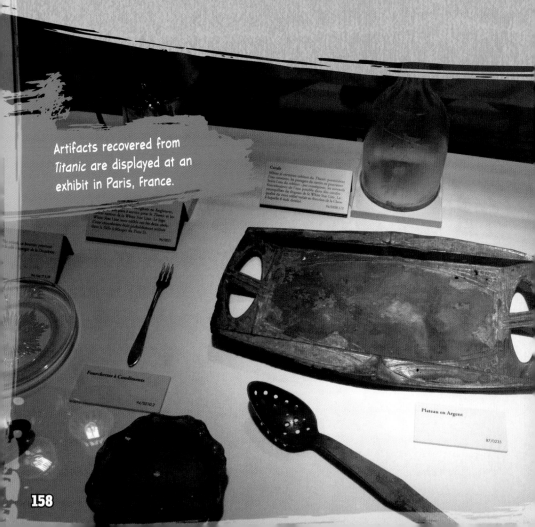

Artifacts recovered from *Titanic* are displayed at an exhibit in Paris, France.

What to Do?

Since *Titanic*'s discovery, many people have weighed in on whether or not people should explore the wreck further.

Preserve It

"**To us it's a grave site – why disturb it any further?**"

— Edward Kamuda, president of the Titanic Historical Society

"**Taking items from *Titanic* is 'grave robbing.'**"

—Eva Hart, *Titanic* survivor

Visit It

"**Most of the people going out there with us have an absolute reverence for *Titanic*.**"

—Rob McCallum, Deep Ocean Expeditions, a diving company

"**If we don't bring them up, years from now, students will ask 'Why? Why when you had the technology, why didn't you do it?'**"

—Robert DiSogra, cofounder of Titanic International Society, a historical group

Eva Hart

Index